A LIFE
REMEMBERED

Karl Böhm

A LIFE
REMEMBERED
MEMOIRS

Translated by
John Kehoe

With an introduction by
Hans Weigel

Marion Boyars
London·New York

First published in Great Britain and the United States in 1992
by MARION BOYARS PUBLISHERS
24 Lacy Road London SW15 1NL
237 East 39th Street, New York, NY 10016

Distributed in the United States and Canada
by Rizzoli International Publications, New York

Published originally in German under the title
Ich erinnere mich ganz genau
by Verlag Fritz Molden, Vienna, in 1970.
© Karlheinz Böhm 1992
© this translation Marion Boyars Publishers 1992

British Library Cataloguing in Publication Data
Böhm, Karl
A life remembered: memoirs.
I. Title   II. [Ich erinnere mich ganz genau.
English]
781.45092

Library of Congress Cataloging in Publication Data
Böhm, Karl, 1894–1981
[Ich erinnere mich ganz genau. English]
A life remembered: memoirs/Karl Böhm; translated by
John Kehoe;
with an introduction by Hans Weigel.
Translation of: Ich erinnere mich ganz genau.
1. Böhm, Karl, 1894–1981.   2. Conductors
(Music)—Biography.
I. Title.
ML422.B73A3   1991
784.2'092—dc20
[B]   91-19526

ISBN 0-7145-2919-2 cloth

Typeset by Ann Buchan (Typesetters) in Baskerville 11/13pt
Printed and bound by Billing & Sons Ltd., Worcester

CONTENTS

KARL BÖHM

A biographical profile by
John Kehoe

Karl Böhm was born on the 28th of August 1894 into a comfortable, middle-class family in Graz, the second city of Austria and capital of Styria. He showed precocious musical talent, but was persuaded by his father to study law as a means of ensuring a livelihood. During the course of his law studies he began working as a coach in the Graz Opera, where he was soon engaged as second conductor. Following a period as a conscript during the First World War, he took his doctorate in law in 1919.

In 1920 he secured the position of first conductor in Graz. He undertook a period of private study with Eusebius Mandyczewski in Vienna, where he not only attended virtually all of the Vienna Philharmonic concerts and productions at the Vienna State Opera, but met the great Wagner conductor Karl Muck, who later recommended him to Bruno Walter. Leaving his secure post in Graz he accepted a less senior position at the Munich State Opera under Bruno Walter and, later, Hans Knappertsbusch. Böhm was then appointed *Generalmusikdirektor* in Darmstadt, where his advocacy of contemporary music, most notably of Alban Berg, first attracted attention. Success at the Hamburg State Opera from 1931 to 1934 was followed by one of the most fruitful periods of his life, in Dresden, where he was to remain until 1943.

It was in Dresden that Böhm created one of the greatest ensembles in the world. He became recognized as a Mozartean of special distinction, and as a Wagner conductor of exceptional clarity. It is his association with Richard Strauss during this period that marks perhaps his greatest contribution. He conducted the first performances of *Die schweigsame Frau* and *Daphne*, which was dedicated to him. Böhm and his wife, the singer Thea Linhard, remained close friends of Richard and Pauline Strauss until their death in 1949.

During the Dresden period, in 1938, Böhm began his association with the Salzburg Festival, where, with the exception of one year after the Second World War, he was to appear annually until prevented by ill-health. It was with the Dresden ensemble, too, that he made his first recordings. He began a close association with the Berlin Philharmonic and, most especially, the Vienna Philharmonic, but the war made guest appearances outside Germany and Austria impossible.

Böhm left Dresden in 1943 to take up the position of Director of the Vienna State Opera until its destruction by American bombing in May 1945. Following the end of the war, although he was never a member of the Nazi party, Böhm's tenure of official posts under the Nazis led to an Allied ban, and he lived for a period on the income from his wife's singing lessons and with the support of friends (including Bruno Walter). Following his reinstatement, he appeared once more at the Salzburg Festival and began to take up guest appearances outside Austria. He directed the German *stagione* at the Teatro Colón, Buenos Aires and appeared at the Metropolitan Opera in New York. He was appointed Director of the Vienna State Opera once again in

1954, but his tenure ended amidst controversy in 1956.

Alongside his reputation as a Mozartean, and his special relationship with the Salzburg Festival and the Vienna Philharmonic, it was Bayreuth that marked some of Böhm's greatest post-war achievements, in collaboration with Wieland Wagner. Recordings of his 1962 *Tristan und Isolde*, with Nilsson, Windgassen and Ludwig, followed by a *Ring* cycle drawn from the 1966 and 1967 performances, remain as testimony to his gifts as a Wagnerian.

The remainder of Karl Böhm's career was centred upon Vienna, Salzburg and Berlin, but with major international guest appearances. Walter Legge invited him to work with the Philharmonia Orchestra, and he became President of the London Symphony Orchestra. Böhm's recording career was long and distinguished, and it reflects the breadth of his achievements: early recordings for EMI-Electrola, Mozart operas (his EMI/Philharmonia *Così fan tutte* is generally recognized as one of the finest of all Mozart recordings), a complete cycle of the Mozart symphonies, Wagner, Richard Strauss, Berg, Beethoven, Schubert for Deutsche Grammofon, with the Decca/Vienna Philharmonic Bruckner 4th Symphony as another pinnacle.

Karl Böhm received practically every honour the musical world could bestow. Among those he particularly cherished were the personal title of General Music Director of Austria, granted by the Austrian State and reserved exclusively to him during his lifetime, and the Freedom of Mozart's city of Salzburg.

Dr Karl Böhm died in Salzburg during the Festival, on 14 August 1981, at the age of 86.

John Kehoe

TRANSLATOR'S NOTE

For the general reader with a lively interest in the musical world, Karl Böhm's memoirs present few demands of a specialist nature. With a few exceptions, I have therefore avoided cluttering up this lively 'read' with elaborate footnotes. For consistency I have quoted titles of musical works in their original language. Names of institutions are given in English translation or in the original, whichever I felt to be the more familiar to the reader.

For one who only rarely saw him conduct, but who treasures many of his recordings, it has been a delight to eavesdrop on his recollections and impressions. I am only too conscious of how little of his very Austrian — very Styrian — personality survives this translation and accept this and other shortcomings as my own.

I should like to thank my good friends Gareth and Gina Lewis for introducing me to the original publication, Conifer Records for allowing me access to their desktop publishing equipment which so eased my task, and Marion Boyars for sharing my belief that Karl Böhm has more English-speaking admirers than he perhaps realized.

John Kehoe

INTRODUCTION

by Hans Weigel

There are conductors, some great ones among them, whom one watches and listens to admiringly, thinking: 'God, that must be hard!' And there are other conductors, among them only the great ones, whom one watches and listens to admiringly, thinking: 'God, that must be easy!' The highest achievement in art is reached when nothing more happens than the work simply being given back what its creator originally gave to it.

Karl Böhm is a grand master of interpretations in the presence of which one tends to think: 'God, that must be easy!' He is a music-maker with God-given talents, endowed with a personality so strong and firmly-founded that it has no need to label itself or to make concessions to the public, and so rich that it can afford not to specialize (or, more correctly, always to specialize in the work or genre to which it is giving voice). Ultimately, he is not merely an opera or concert conductor, specializing in the classics or the new, in Mozart, Beethoven, Brahms, Wagner, Bruckner, Strauss or Berg. He is at home not within any specific area, but in Music itself. And this versatility is all the more pleasurable and admirable in that it encompasses Mozart, who has been recognized and fully understood only in our century, a composer to whom few conductors of yesterday and today have really been capable of doing full justice, and whom, Karl Böhm, as one (after Bruno Walter and Richard Strauss) called and chosen in our time, knows how to serve.

Conducting is only a difficult trade when one cannot accomplish or master it 'playfully' and succeeds all the more perfectly the less visibly it is done. Many a great conductor stands or sits at the podium almost motionless, casually overseeing the end result which he has worked towards in rehearsals and previous performances.

Karl Böhm is too active, too burdened with temperament, to remain quite so static. Also, he is too fond of conducting, and while conducting appearing not to. Not every conductor likes conducting; many suffer, many endure, many are angry while exercising their profession. Karl Böhm, however, is full of positive energies and fulfils himself with enthusiasm, inwardly and outwardly, mentally and artistically when he finds himself on the podium. He loves not only music but also what he may do for it — and this love must live itself out in the most extreme, the highest and most sublime of visible, earthly forms.

That he enjoys conducting so much is related to his approach to his chosen profession, and this is a very Austrian state of affairs. For productive Austrians prefer to reach for the stars from where they are most at home but not where they have gone to school; that is, beyond the prescribed hierarchies of a profession learned for the everyday world. They have prepared for one thing but do something else. If somebody asks them as a child: 'What do you want to be, my lad?' they will not name that activity which will later make them famous.

Karl Böhm learned the piano, composition and musical theory. He did not learn to be a conductor, he was one from the start. And because he took up the practice of it without

any special schoolmasterly, theoretical preparation, he retains
in his work the freshness and immediacy of an adventure, a
successful experiment. Sadly he does not compose or play the
piano because he was too systematically trained in these arts.
He does not know what great art there is in his conducting,
because it comes to him naturally.

The Austrian gods — Styrian Department — blessed·
him with the gifts of a great music-maker to embrace the
highest, the most difficult, the most complicated and
technically intractable music: from a Strauss waltz to the
5/8- 7/7- and 13/8 bar in *Wozzeck* he has built a great
bridge. The most difficult music of all is not the most
complicated but Mozart, in fact, because one feels particularly humble and self-conscious before him. When Karl
Böhm plays Mozart with the Vienna Philharmonic, a
pinnacle is reached which touches the absolute in an almost
suspicious and impermissible manner.

Karl Böhm was not schooled in the writing of books, nor is
he, surprisingly, a natural-born writer. As the need to write
his 'Memoirs' became acute, he faced the classic dilemma
of all those who have something to say but who do not
belong to the future of writing: ought one dare to set foot in
a new terrain as a dilettante, or should one use the formula
'as-told-to' common in the Anglo-Saxon countries? When
the great man A has something to say, he tells it to a
professional, Z, who makes a book out of it which is then
called 'Impressions Recalled' by A 'as told to' Z. Such a
combination of a personality with a practised stylist is not
always a happy one. If I am involved in this book, there is,
however, no question of it being in such a manner; for I did
not want to become a cross between a hairdresser and a
megaphone but only a catalyst.

By happy chance I was having lunch one day with Frau

Ruth Binde of Diogenes Verlag in the Kronenhalle in Zurich and we spotted Mr and Mrs Karlheinz Böhm a few tables away. Karlheinz Böhm had just been discussing his father's long-overdue 'Memoirs', and I told him of how the Werner Krauss book, *The Theatre of my Life*, had come about and gladly expressed my readiness to use the same method with my revered Dr Karl Böhm.

So it was, through his son, that in December 1967 I spent several hours in Dr Böhm's apartment in Wien-Grinzing. I sat opposite him and tried to make him forget that behind him was sitting the lady who had also sat with Werner Krauss in Porzellangasse, Vienna IX, taking shorthand. So a typescript emerged the authenticity of which outweighed what it lacked in literary brilliance. To cast it into book form took nothing more than what is done editorially with any text transferred from the spoken to the written medium.

What is presented here — apart from a few inessential retouchings — is what Karl Böhm said; the reader too is seated opposite him in the Grinzing apartment and receives, with great immediacy, Karl Böhm's recollections and opinions in his own words. A great deal has been written about him already, but what there is to be said of him should be by him, and he associates himself readily with this view.

The book's title was already clear to me: Karl Böhm, while he was talking, used (quite unconsciously) variants on the phrase *'Ich erinnere mich ganz genau'* (*I recall exactly*'). I brought this *Leitmotiv* to his attention and was quietly happy when it came round again. Thus did this text find a kind of form. One could describe it, like *Till Eulenspiegel*, as a kind of rondo: a rondo of recollections and experiences in a great life of musical activity.

H.W., Vienna, February 1968

CHAPTER ONE

Graz, Schulgasse 17 — 'Min' — My two great-
uncles — First music lessons — Studies in Vienna —
Caruso — The War — Starting out in Graz —
Fidelio, my opera of destiny

Although I really took it for granted, from the moment I
first began to think that I would become a musician, my
good father, who later made every effort to support my
musical studies, firmly wished for me to take a doctorate in
law. This was because he, as a lawyer and syndic of the
Graz State Theatre, had come a great deal into contact
with singers and other artists and knew the misery of
artistic mediocrity: 'These people not only earn less money
than the "successful" ones', he said, 'they also spend their
lives desperately unhappy since they attribute the blame for
their failure not to any lack of talent but to the double-
dealing of their colleagues or bad luck — of which there is
no such thing in art.

'When I feel that you really will achieve something great,
you can count upon my full support. But you must serve
your time studying law as a fall-back, so that you can come
into my office when it all goes wrong.'

Not long ago, on All Saints Day, I visited my parents'
grave once again. It is in the cemetery at Steinfelden; just a

few steps away is the last resting-place of the great conductor Karl Muck, one of my patrons, who was married to the daughter of Dr Ferdinand Portugall, the mayor of Graz. Dr Portugall had done a great deal for art in the city and was a Freeman of Graz. And still — although he had been Mayor and Freeman — nobody had bothered about his grave. That has always made me angry. Later, through a friend of mine who was deputy mayor, I saw to it that it came under the care of the Graz city authorities. At my last visit I was again able to confirm that the last resting places of two great men were looked after in a worthy manner.

On the way back from the graves of my parents and my younger brother Walter — he was one of the most highly-regarded doctors in Graz and deeply attached to music — I had a strong impulse: I had to visit the house where I was born, No 17 Schulgasse, a small house near the inner city, not very grand, in imitation Nuremberg style. Next door still stood the inn *Zu den drei Hacken*, to which, when my father bought the house, there was a bakery attached. The baker's shop belonged to my father's father, who had immigrated from Eger.

On my father's side, therefore, I am of German Bohemian origin, on my mother's side from French Alsatians. My mother's grandfather spoke only French and was a woodcarver; an artist who preferred religious themes such as madonnas more than anything else.

I entered the house. There is quite a large garden, to which many of my childhood memories are linked. Then, as I went upstairs, I saw that everything that had once been beautiful in this house had fallen victim to decay. A young man was coming down the stairs — my brother had sold the house ten years before — and told me, after I had introduced myself, that it was his intention to turn the house into a superior kind of pension. It still had the fine stucco ceilings representing the four seasons. The heirs of the present owner had found that the place was too costly, the site too dear, and soon after my visit, the house was torn down. So that was in fact my last visit to the house of my birth, for in those days the children were born at home; my mother had brought us three boys into the world in my parents' bedroom.

The first thing I noticed as I went up was a passage about which my mother had written in a carefully-kept diary, which is now sadly lost. In this book she clearly recorded how I developed from the time I opened my eyes up to my second year.

My first word was not 'Mama' or 'Papa' as is usual. Instead I said '*Min*', and '*Min*' was my word for music. By that I meant not just the nearby church, from which the sound of the organ could occasionally be heard, but above all the Dominican barracks a few steps away. It was a barracks like any other, except that every day at a certain hour the regimental band would pass by. I raised my finger and cried '*Min*' without saying anything else, until my mother finally grasped what I wanted. She picked me up, went with me to the window so that I could hear the music better, and I repeated, '*Min*'. And so music was the first element in my life.

An Englishwoman who taught my mother English cast my horoscope; you can believe what you like, but still, she really did predict my career.

My walk through my parents' old house led me on to the balcony, which was originally wide open but which my father later had covered over and rebuilt. Once more memories came flooding back. I clung to my mother's skirts: she could never go far without my crying terribly and had to put her coat on in the bathroom so that I might not see that she was going out. Finally she hit upon the idea of engaging the very best hurdy-gurdy man — there was still a large number of them in Graz. She put a crown in his hand, that was an almost princely fee, and said to him: 'Go to No. 17 Schulgasse, where there's a little boy sitting on a stool waiting for me to come back.' That worked; the man played on his hurdy-gurdy until my mother came home again. I had stopped crying.

I also had a vivid recollection of a terrible occurrence as I made my way through the house: my father, who was rather overweight, had had a home steam-bath put in. It was fed by a petrol or oil stove, and one went into a box to sweat. Once, after we had gone to bed, the apparatus caught fire. We leapt out of bed and, together with my mother, tore the whole thing apart. Nothing had happened to my father, but one could see the burn marks on the floor for a long time afterwards. In the same room I swotted for my school-leaving certificate. With a friend I learned mathematics, a subject for which I simply had no gift whatever. By chance I had found out what one of my test problems was to be. My friend was a brilliant mathematician — I was out of my depth — and he explained the exercise to me. I still didn't understand it. So what did I do? I learned it by heart, like a parrot. When it turned up in the exam, I began writing out the formulas so quickly that my teacher looked on amazed, but when it came to giving the answer I was stuck. Fortunately the headmaster said, 'the boy is over-excited' — because everything was absolutely right up to that point — and so I passed.

I had one more very clear childhood memory. We had in our family two famous great-uncles; one was the last Austro-Hungarian War Minister and, although he was a fine, upright man and soldier, I didn't get on with him, because I hate war. The second famous relation, Carl Link, was an uncle of my father's, and the successor of a tenor called Wachtel who was as famous in his day as Caruso became later. I have since found his picture. He was the first German-speaking Don José at the Berlin Court Opera*, studied medicine and derived such pleasure from his voice that, as my father often told us, he would get up in the morning and sing a high C with full voice in his nightshirt in front of the mirror. He had hardly any singing lessons and remained a lifelong natural singer, which of course did nothing to help the length of his career. He was a splendid Arnold in Rossini's *William Tell*. After Berlin he was engaged for a long time in Stuttgart, but he was such a hothead that he had a fight with the Intendant† a year before his retirement, got no pension and as an old man had to eke out a miserable existence by giving singing lessons.

My father had a beautiful baritone voice — between baritone and tenor, really. I accompanied him on the piano when I was only eight. He always had to transpose the tenor parts which he preferred, but once he succeeded in singing the stretta from *Il Trovatore* in B major, using a poker as a sword. He took singing lessons with my uncle, who by then had a feeble, cracked voice but nevertheless sang us a few of his old opera arias. The singing lessons always took place after supper. I was allowed to get into my mother's bed — my parents' bedroom was next to the

---

* *Hofoper, Staatsoper*, etc. At the fall of the Hohenzollern and Hapsburg monarchies in 1919 the institutions which had been designated *Hofoper* (Court Opera) became *Staatsoper* (State Opera). The author occasionally refers to institutions by their pre-1919 name when referring to later events, however, and I have restored consistency in such cases. (Tr)

† In German opera houses the *Intendant* (or *Generalintendant*) is the chief executive, with overall authority for both artistic and administrative matters — the term implies more than simply 'theatre manager'. The *Generalmusikdirektor* (usually abbreviated to *GMD*) is the highest authority on musical matters. Occasionally the two posts are combined: the Directorship of the Vienna State Opera, for example, has on occasion combined both roles and, since the establishment is answerable to the Federal Government, this can become a politically sensitive appointment. (Tr)

music salon — to listen from there. Those were lovely times, and when I had drifted off to sleep I was carried to my bed, still asleep.

I started piano lessons early on, with a teacher whose name I won't mention because he was well-intentioned towards me, but did everything possible to rob a young person of any joy in music. That he was unable to take it away from me is just one proof of my indestructible love of music. He was always saying 'You don't practise enough!' and then he would show me two purulent finger nails with the words, 'You must practise for as long as it takes for you to have purulent nails too.'

Then I went·to a fine lady piano teacher who recognized my talent and at the end of the lessons would play with me four-handed music from Weber operas, later from *Lohengrin* and *Der fliegende Holländer*. The great inspiration came, however, from my teacher Franz Weiss. My dear, unforgettable Franz Weiss was a schoolmaster and choirmaster of the Graz Male Choir. He had an extraordinarily wide musical education and was good with young people. He married one of the richest heiresses in Graz; practically half of the Rosenberg, an area in Graz, belonged to his wife. So he did not need to give lessons and only took pupils who it gave him pleasure to teach. To this man I owe the most fruitful encouragement during my time as a grammar school boy. He also helped out, just for the pure artistic pleasure, as second harpist in the Graz Stadttheater and invited me to attend the rehearsals. Just imagine: a schoolmaster who says to a schoolboy, 'Better come to the rehearsal, you'll learn more there than in school!' I didn't need telling twice. I handed my school satchel to a grocer and went to the rehearsals for *Der Rosenkavalier* which at that time was being given its first performance in Graz, not long after its Dresden première. So my parents were really surprised when they saw in my half-yearly school report eighty-five lessons missed without leave.

After taking my school leaving certificate in 1913 I was able, thanks to my father's generosity, to go to Vienna for a year. And I must just add something here: my father knew all of the artists in Graz well, including the conductors in the Graz State Theatre. One day the conductor of Marschner's *Hans Heiling* fell ill and the Director said to my father, 'My principal conductor has a temperature, and the house is sold out. What am I to do?' There was a young conductor engaged at the theatre who only conducted burlesque and operettas, Franz Schalk. My father suggested, 'Schalk is a very gifted musician, he ought to conduct,' and he called in the young man. He studied the score overnight and took over the performance. That was the beginning of his great career — he became principal conductor in Graz, later came to Vienna in the same capacity where, to crown his career, he became Director of the Vienna State Opera, at first alongside Richard Strauss.

Schalk never forgot that it was my father who gave him his first push, as it were, in his career. He reciprocated when I became a music student and advised me not to go to the Academy but to take private lessons with Eusebius Mandyczewski, the long-serving archivist of the *Gesellschaft der Musikfreunde** in Vienna. I went to see him, he liked me and he took me on as a private pupil. In one year I learned from him what would have taken three years at the

* The 'Society of the Friends of Music', which was established in Vienna in 1812, founded a conservatoire in 1817. Its home is the Vienna Musikverein, where its valuable archive is housed, and where it organizes prestigious orchestral and chamber music concerts. The Great Hall of the Musikverein (the Musikvereinsaal) has become familiar to an international audience through the televized New Year's Day Concerts with the Vienna Philharmonic. (Tr)

Academy; that period with Mandyczewski was the most fruitful of my time as a student. I never had just a one-hour lesson with him, it was always an hour and a half. I studied with him the whole of counterpoint and harmony, and had to bring a composition to every lesson. Gradually, reading a score became something taken for granted.

Apart from that I had five or six hours of piano with Groer. At that time I was determined to become a pianist. I had already accompanied singers at the Stephanie-Saal in Graz, playing Schubert Impromptus and Chopin in between — and enjoyed good reviews.

My teacher Mandyczewski gave me broad encouragement: only he couldn't get on with modern music. After the first performance of *Elektra* — he was so good-hearted with his little cap and his beard — he said to me: 'Tell me, is it possible to get into this music? I can't follow it! Isn't that right, it starts off with someone beating someone else over the head, then there's a brief peaceful interval (Orestes' scene) and then the next character comes in and beats someone else over the head?' He had been Brahms' most intimate friend, and Brahms' works had passed through his hands before going off to be engraved.

Alongside my musical studies I had enrolled for law. Today I am an Honorary Senator of Graz University, but I have to confess that I never entered the Graz lecture rooms before my examinations — that is to say, I had indeed attended lectures, but not on law.

I remember doing music history in Vienna with Guido Adler. His lectures, which captivated me, were the only ones I attended regularly. May the jurists of Graz forgive me!

Thanks to my father's generosity I had a subscription to the Vienna State Opera. I often went to the Burgtheater too. I decided according to the cast lists — if they weren't first-class, I preferred to see the performances at the

Burgtheater. Harry Walden and Josef Kainz used to perform there: the latter I saw twice as Hamlet and once as Mark Antony.

Caruso made a guest appearance in Vienna in 1910 — never in Graz, because his fee was then 15,000 Kronen, which is in terms of today's purchasing power around $60,000. I got very angry at the time — I was a very young man. 'It's scandalous that anyone should get such a fee', but then, when I had heard him sing, I said, 'that is far too little, the man is beyond price!' He sang Radamès, and the Viennese were somewhat disappointed, because of course they were used to Leo Slezak, whose voice was far more dramatic. Slezak was at the performance that evening and the next day sang Des Grieux in Massenet's *Manon* with Caruso and Carl Burian in the audience. In the following performance, Burian sang Tristan, and then Caruso had his greatest success as Rodolfo in *La Bohème*.

I heard him in the course of two or three seasons, twice as Don José, as the Duke in *Rigoletto* — he was vocally unsurpassable — then in *Un Ballo in Maschera*, *I Pagliacci*, *La Fanciulla del West* and in *Tosca*. He was as great an actor as he was a singer, all the actors at the Burgtheater confirmed this. I remember exactly every gesture Caruso made, I could describe every vocal nuance. His voice was as soft as velvet, without any hard edges, and he covered the break with ease. In the difficult duet with Micaëla in *Carmen* one had the feeling that he was under no strain whatsoever. He never sang from the footlights and never for a second longer than the composer had written. He was of course a national idol in Italy, but never as beloved in Italy as in Austria, Germany and France, and most of all at the Met in New York.

I have a particularly vivid memory of *Carmen*. The end of the third Act was an enormous success for Caruso. When, with a cry like a wild animal, he stabbed Carmen, it had a hitherto unmatched expressive power. In any case he had a congenial partner, Marie Gutheil-Schoder, for me the best Carmen in the world, although she really had little voice. I can still see her on the stage as if it were yesterday — she had a wonderful figure, very slender, not really a beautiful face, but it became beautiful through her art as an actress. When this woman — I can recall exactly what she wore, a white blouse, yellow skirt, white stockings and red shoes — began slowly to tap her feet in the habanera; that was really stirring and radiated eroticism. As I recall her, I cannot help comparing her with Marlene Dietrich.

Caruso performed the end of *Carmen* — a parallel with the famous Wagner singer and producer Albert Niemann, who threw himself on the ground at the end of the Pilgrims' Chorus and kissed the earth — in an unusual way. He did not stab Carmen, but on the spot where Don José had thrown down the ring drew a flick knife and said, cold as ice, 'so now, die', while still pursuing her. Before she runs to the bullring he let the blade flash out, holding the knife in front of himself, and she runs on to it.

Naturally I went to all the Philharmonic concerts. The conductor Felix von Weingartner made a great impression on me. Earlier, I had attended concerts in Vienna, while I was still at school, through a schoolfriend of my father, who had close connections with the Philharmonic. Sadly, I never heard Gustav Mahler.

One day — I was on my way back to Vienna from an air display, the people in the street were shouting something that I hadn't heard before. 'Extra, extra, Crown Prince and wife murdered in Sarajevo!' screamed the headlines. At that my stay in Vienna came to an abrupt end: I had to return to Graz.

I came home on the first of July. The situation was highly precarious; people were talking about a possible war. One evening we were sitting with friends in Windisch-

Feistritz in their vineyard, which was on a hill. All of a sudden we saw the light of a lamp coming slowly nearer with an eery, swaying movement. I clearly recall the arrival of the messenger who informed my father's friend: 'War has just broken out!' Austria had declared war on Serbia and announced mobilization. My school mates were worse off than I, because they had already volunteered for a year's duty; they had to go back immediately and were sent to the front right away.

My father was as much against war and an anti-militarist as I, while my mother displayed great enthusiasm for Kaiser Wilhelm, although she was otherwise a most unwarlike woman. My father had advised me to do everything I could to avoid being called up. But I was a fully fit young man, and it was hard for me not to be 'accepted'. So I was declared fit for service. I was very keen — for, since my earliest youth I had been a passionately keen rider (first on a donkey, then we had a pony in a villa near Graz, then a horse as well) — to be posted to a mounted troop. In those days the warrior had to bring a horse for his country, then he was allowed to go into the cavalry. The selection panel asked, 'Where do you want to go?' 'Into the artillery,' I said. 'All full.' 'Into the cavalry,' I said. 'All full.' I assured them that I could provide a horse. 'Then you can only go into a supply division,' they replied. I went straight away to my father in his office. 'Accepted?' Father asked. 'Yes, fit for duty.' 'Oh, Lord! Which troop?' 'Supply Division'. 'Very good. They look after the supply line, you'll always get something to eat there.'

We drove to our villa at Baierdorf near Graz, which also had a large orchard and wood. My mother was already there. She asked me: 'Are you passed fit for service?' 'Yes.' 'Fine, where?' 'Supply Division.' 'What, those are real whip-crackers!' 'Look', my father declared, 'I much prefer the blue of their tunic to the red of the Artillery's.'

To cut a long story short, I had to enlist right away. I was born in 1894 and 20 years old by then, the best age for cannon fodder. I went to the Supply Division in Graz, which was the favourite of the Jews. I had nothing but Jewish friends there — it was moving that later, after all the horrible events and experiences of the 'Third Reich' five of those soldier comrades in New York rang up and asked, 'Karl, how are you then?' I got on very well in this outfit, except that a few of the corporals hounded us, as so many military superiors consider it their duty to do. We had a First Lieutenant too: he was rather fat, a minor civil servant from the country, and was by then a big noise as a lieutenant in the reserve.

One day it was terribly hot. We were doing idiotic exercises and drill, and I asked to be allowed a drink of water, to which the Lieutenant replied 'Back straight, knees bend, and hop to the fountain', which was about three hundred metres away. So I hopped. As I got there, he ordered, 'about turn!' and I had to hop back without having had a drink. I wanted to kill him!

I was, as I have said, passionately keen on horse-riding, and have ridden bareback. The horse I had brought with me into the army was called Nepomuk. He was very big and a very hard ride. Even when trotting you had to have a very firm grip with the knees if you were not to be thrown from the saddle. The First Lieutenant had me on the long rein and amused himself by hitting me over the calves with it. 'You have a bad knee-grip', he said. 'That's because Nepomuk is a very high stepper', I replied. 'Dismount, I shall show you.' The First Lieutenant mounted the horse and dug his spurs into his flanks. My good Nepomuk would not put up with that, he reared and the First Lieutenant fell flat on his face in a puddle by the barracks gate.

Soon I became a corporal, then troop commander. As such I was in charge of the stable guard. We had baggage horses, as well as the officers' horses. I came into the stable one midnight. The sentry was totally drunk, and following regulations, I had to yell at him, 'you drunken lout . . .' as is customary in the military. At that a Pinzgauer horse woke up and kicked out. I was caught and fell senseless — and I finally woke up in my own bed in 17 Schulgasse. The doctor confirmed a heavy loss of blood — incidentally, the spot still hurts today — and a not unserious contusion. I lay there with an icebag and thought as I got better: 'It would be a pity to die a hero's death; how can I fix things once I get up? How do I get out of the military?'

I had an angel for a regimental doctor — a general practitioner, Dr Mitterer, who had had to enlist in the course of the war. I shall never forget him. On the basis of my accident he certified me C – suitable for home duties only. I was therefore useful only 'in serious circumstances' and had to carry out minor duties around the office. There we mostly made silly jokes, especially concerning a First Lieutenant, a nobleman, whose Adjutant I was. I said to one of my comrades: 'I bet you he'd sign his own death warrant' — a comment for which, impudent dog, I could have been executed. So I wrote: 'By decree of . . .' — I knew the form — 'First Lieutenant So-and-so is to be shot.' He actually signed it.

During my convalescence I had begun studying. Then I went to a crammer and took my first state examination, which was in fact relatively easy, in Graz. Also I had the urge to compose, and there emerged one song after another.

A Master of Horse of Bohemian origin once caught me writing down notes: 'A miserable music-scribbler, are you? You shall hear from me!' And a few days later the Adjutant said to me: 'Your orders for active service are through, you have to go to the front.' Then I wrote a pleading letter to my great-uncle, the War Minister. My two brothers were at the front as a Lieutenant and First Lieutenant and were in all the battles at Doberdo. So they were heroes, as opposed to myself. I asked my great-uncle to let my commanding officer know that I was none other than his great-nephew. That he did, but I knew nothing of it: I only learned that the Master of Horse had said to my Adjutant: 'That one-year volunteer Böhm really is a nice lad, he is to report to me today.' And he said to me, 'how are you?' And I answered: 'We have so much to do.' You can imagine what a cheek that was. I was then sent to a barracks just outside Graz and had to carry out a few exercises with my men which consisted mostly of sunbathing. The men were very fond of me, as they usually had to do only two hours' duty.

One day my great-uncle came to Graz. I knew that my Master of Horse always went to the Café Kaiserhof in the afternoons and so I strolled with my great-uncle over to the said café, where we stepped through the door arm-in-arm. The Master of Horse leapt up, I nodded a casual greeting — that was my greatest military triumph!

The war was getting worse and worse. Then I got bronchitis, and the doctor, with whom I had become very friendly and for whom I always played the piano, certified that I was a suspected TB case. It was, of course, a totally exaggerated statement. They even asked me: 'Are you seeking compensation?' Because, for illnesses brought on in the course of military service, one could get compensation. Of course, I refused and was dismissed from the army as completely unfit, without compensation. That was in 1916.

I had a colleague, Georg Markowitz, a conductor of above-average gifts, who asked me one day: 'Wouldn't you like to come into the theatre with us?' That was fine by me. They were in the middle of rehearsals of *Zar und Zimmermann*, and I played the piano for a chorus rehearsal of the cantata from the third Act. It must have been ghastly. I knew the Wagner and Mozart operas pretty well, but at that time found Lortzing — incidentally Strauss felt the same — utterly beneath my dignity. Despite that, however, they gave me a contract as a *répétiteur* for which I give thanks to the 'kindly musical gods!'

Two days after I joined the Graz Opera, Markowitz fell ill, and I had to take on all the stage work for *Aïda*. That was a great deal then, much harder than today, when everything is much more specialized. Since I had never had conducting lessons, in the stage *banda*'s triumphal march in the second Act I beat the second beat of the four-four to the right instead of to the left, which set off a proper revolution in the *banda* which only my kindly Director was able to quell.

At that time Grevenberg — he was a good-hearted man — had taken over the theatre in Graz as Director and brought a famous conductor to Graz: Oskar C. Posa. His conducting was a bit clumsy but he took a rehearsal of *Ariadne auf Naxos* such as I have seldom experienced.

I remember quite clearly, too, a performance of *Das Rheingold*. The low E-flat in the double basses is supported by an organ pedal note. That was too boring for me: just sitting there with my foot on the pedal. This joker put a stone on the pedal, and in the meantime flirted with one of the ballerinas and the low E-flat went on sounding, while I was 'otherwise engaged', and the Rhine Maidens started singing. As soon as I heard this, I clambered in record time back on to the organ bench and, just a fraction too late, released the E-flat from the stone. So I got myself out of hot water, otherwise I should have rightly had a real dressing-down from Posa.

I rehearsed everything really, from the bottom up. Markowitz had to accompany a few couplets in the *Die Trutzige* by Anzengruber. 'That would be something for you,' he said, and I took over the accompaniment — with a risibly small orchestra. I can remember that occasion as if it were yesterday: an actress came to me and said: 'I am hoarse today, Herr Kapellmeister, I'll have to sing down a third.' I replied that I did not know whether my team of geniuses could do that just on sight, but I went to the rostrum and shortly before the curtain went up asked them to play the couplet down a third. A few called out that they could only transpose down a tone: but it was too late for discussion, and we began with some in B major, others in A major! I still don't know how we got back together again.

My first appearance as a conductor, however, had taken place five weeks before the event just described. We had played *Er und seine Schwester* by Bernhard Buchbinder, and in the piece there is a chorus of seamstresses. I wrote about it in my diary, which is sadly lost: 'Choir totally thrown. Whose fault? The conductor's!'

Suddenly, because the Director liked me, and as recompense for my gigantic efforts as *répétiteur*, I was given my first opera. It was performed on October 17, 1917 and, if I exclude the preceding minor events, I celebrated my fiftieth anniversary as a conductor on October 17, 1967. On this date I conducted my first opera, *Der Trompeter von Säckingen*, about which the critic Decsey wrote: 'The opera will, I predict, be struck out of his contract by every General Music Director.' Uncut, the opera would last five hours. I reduced it to two-and-a-half hours, otherwise it would have been unbearable. The score was so fat that one had to bind together the cut sections, or else one would have turned to the wrong page. The part of Marie on that occasion was sung by Anni Münchow, who had originally been an operetta singer. At that time she was also singing *Die lustige Witwe*, had a top C and C sharp and even moved on later, via the Marie in *Der Trompeter von Säckingen*, to *Elektra*. Adolf Permann, a magnificent baritone, sang the Trumpeter. It was an enormous success. Today it's impossible to listen to this sing-song opera.

I was very attached to the Graz opera house, where I

received so many lasting impressions. But I heard the first opera of my life in the Theater am Franzensplatz, the other large theatre in Graz, at my mother's side. It was *Fidelio* — incidentally, the first score that my parents gave me as a present.

After *Der Trompeter von Säckingen* I was given another opera, one which still means a great deal to me today; *Der Freischütz*.

Alongside rehearsing singers and three evenings a week on duty I had — with the help of a crammer — taken the second state law examination. With my feet up like an American, tearing and biting countless handkerchiefs, I studied Law at night — Constitutional Law, Penal Law, Trial Law, Civil Law and Civil Process, Competition and Exchange Law — till two and two-thirty in the morning. Still I got up on time and was in the theatre by ten o'clock. In this period, when I was already busy as an opera conductor, came the second *viva voce* and then the third state examination.

By then I had the feeling that I had a contribution to make to artistic life and asked myself why I should go on studying law. I had to struggle with myself, with a great deal of inner resistance, in order not to give up three-quarters of the way along the road.

At the third *viva voce* they first put questions to me about the Geneva Convention. Professor Lenz, a delightful and lovable man, who already knew me from the theatre — later, he often used to come to my opera performances in Vienna and to my concerts — talked to me only about the theatre. At the end, coming back to the Geneva Convention, he put the question to me: 'What was the treatment of prisoners-of-war like?' 'Bad,' I replied, from experience of a recently-ended world war. 'That's fine,' he said. I got my 'Satisfactory' grade and passed. Whenever I met him later in Graz on the Schlossberg or somewhere, he would always say: 'What was the treatment of prisoners-of-war like?', and I would always answer: 'Bad.' 'Good, good,' he would say.

I took my doctorate on 4 April 1919 at the Karl-Franz University in Graz. At the ceremony, at which almost the entire personnel of the opera was present, the Rector gave a very witty speech in which he said, among other things, that he was in the unusual position of granting a doctorate in law to a musician. I still remember clearly that shortly afterwards I was conducting *Der fliegende Holländer* in the Graz Stadttheater. Luckily I was never let loose on humanity as a Doctor of Law, and my progress as an artist soon made rapid strides forward.

In 1920 came the 150th anniversary of the birth of Beethoven. I had had such great success as a conductor that the Director — although there was a Director of Opera in Graz — promised me one of Beethoven's greatest works. The opera *Fidelio* and the Ninth Symphony were performed in the Graz Opera House — but the Director of Opera had first choice. He decided on the Ninth, and I got *Fidelio*. My first *Fidelio* — on Beethoven's 150th birthday.

At the performance of the Ninth Symphony the Director behaved disgracefully — what drove him to it I do not know. I recall that he had his baton — like the head of John the Baptist to Salome — presented to him on a silver salver. Then there was a 'mishap' in the Scherzo, and they had to start again from the beginning. The whole event laboured under an unlucky star and was treated accordingly in the press.

Three days later I conducted *Fidelio* and was fortunate enough to have a great success with it. Ernst Decsey wrote a review that began with the words: *'That* was a Beethoven Celebration' and concluded with the words 'That was *the* Beethoven Celebration.'

After this first victory I had free rein in Graz. The Director of Opera treated me as if *I* were the Director, and offered me this position for the coming season. But in the 1920/21 season I was already able to conduct whatever I wanted. I chose *Tristan und Isolde, Walküre* and, in the concert hall, the then new *Alpensymphonie* by Richard Strauss. I played it together with Beethoven's Fifth, and looking back, I have to say, that it was a grisly combination! The two pieces of music really have nothing in common. My only excuse is that I wanted to conduct both works — for the first time, of course.

The concert had such a response, however, that it had to be repeated twice. The second performance was at the same time my farewell to Graz. The concerts took place in the Stephanie-Saal, and I remember that my admirers covered the whole conductor's rostrum with alpine flowers.

CHAPTER TWO

Munich — 'Where are the clarinets?' —
Friendship with Bruno Walter —
From Wagner to Mozart — Frau Thea —
Ariadne without rehearsal — The haunted Director
— Shots in the Feldherrnhalle

In Graz I also conducted a new production of *Otello*. At the
dress rehearsal, before the start of the third Act, I received
a telegram in which Bruno Walter invited me to come to
the Munich Opera under contract to conduct in the
position of third or fourth conductor. Two trial operas were
planned: *Freischütz* and *Madama Butterfly*. With my thoughts
on Munich I continued the rehearsal, went home, told my
parents nothing about it and spent a night considering
what to do. I have to say it was not an easy thing to make a
final decision. I had in my hands the post of Director of
Opera in Graz for the coming year and that was something
most unusual for a young man of my age. Should I risk a
conducting trial at the Munich National Theatre? In the
end I decided to put my firm engagement at risk — for to
fail in Munich would have damaged my position in Graz —
and to go to Munich and conduct these two operas. The
train connections were very bad in those days. I travelled
with my brother Walter, later a doctor. We had to make an

overnight stop at Bischofshofen, change three times — and on top of that I had a large boil and a lot of pain as a result. I arrived in Munich totally worn out.

I did not see Bruno Walter at all. I spoke to the General Manager of the theatre and got one hour for the *Freischütz* rehearsal. In just this one hour — I rehearsed principally the Finale of the last Act — I got to know the orchestra. I can still remember clearly, at the point where the Hermit enters and sings the words to Ottokar: 'Speak thou his sentence' the two clarinets have to play together with the two oboes, but the clarinets remained silent. I said in all modesty to the first clarinet, a fat Munich man called Wagner, 'where are the clarinets, then?' To which he replied, crossly: 'We've nothing to play there.' I said: 'In my score there are two clarinets.' 'Not in my part,' he answered. Here I have to add that these orchestral parts had been used since the first performance of *Freischütz* in Munich; the parts were by then so old that you could still see the stains from the oil lamps which used to light the music stands. I called for the orchestra attendant and asked him to bring me the theatre's copy of the score, in which there were also two clarinets. I showed it to Herr Wagner, and suddenly someone clapped me on the shoulder. 'Good, bravo,' I heard. And with that I had won over the orchestra, since the bravos came from none other than Bruno Walter.

The part of Max in *Freischütz* was sung by Karl Erb, and Agathe was Delia Reinhardt, who had a wonderful lyric soprano voice. I got good reviews, but heard nothing from Bruno Walter.

Three days later came *Madama Butterfly* (incidentally, the Munich State Opera gave me these two programme sheets for my seventieth birthday). But on this evening nothing happened. I closed the score — the public was quite nice to me and applauded the young conductor, but that's all there was. I spent a sleepless night. Finally the telephone call came from the Director's office. I was to come to the theatre. Bruno Walter came up to me and asked: 'Now, my dear colleague, how do you like Munich?' I said: 'I like Munich very much indeed.' Then Bruno Walter replied: 'Munich likes you very much, too.'

I always had a good relationship with Bruno Walter. We wrote to each other even during the war, and our friendship endured for a lifetime. I told him that I had conducted *Fidelio* in Graz, upon which he retorted, 'you won't conduct that here for a while, but I do think that you can learn something with me.' I concurred with him, and then he said something that I have always found confirmed in the course of my life. 'My dear young friend, I have had the bitter experience' (he had been shamefully treated by the critics in Vienna — after *Lohengrin* they had advised him to take up another profession) 'that in our career every step forward has to be paid for terribly. This step forward has to be made up threefold. I would advise you — not for my own purposes,' he added, 'to stay here. You will work your way up and learn much. Take the position in Munich.' I found him sympathetic at first sight and I resolved to accept his invitation. The whole of Graz went into a spin, that I should be committing such an idiocy. But I was not to be deflected. I conducted the *Tristan* and took up my appointment in Munich in the early summer of 1921.

At the start I had to conduct operas about which I had no idea: *Martha* and *Un Ballo in Maschera*. My repertoire was still relatively small, since I had only one or two years' practical opera experience behind me. So once again there were nights of study just as before with my law exams, but more fruitful, since this was material that corresponded to my gifts and my first love.

One thing was decisive above all else, however: Bruno Walter brought me closer to Mozart. I came from a family atmosphere in which Richard Wagner was deified. My mother was incredibly musical, not just a music-lover, while my father was a music-lover but not musical in the real sense of the word. He found it difficult to learn new songs; for example, Strauss's *Heimliche Aufforderung* which I had to teach him. And there were no other musical gods for him before Richard Wagner. Looking back, I find it astonishing how this magician Wagner had seized such a man, who came from a baker's family, originally had nothing to do with music and only became a passionate Wagnerian after his first experience of a Wagner performance. At that time, with the battles for Wagner, this was indeed important; there was need of Wagnerians then. My father was one of the first visitors to Bayreuth, too. He became friendly with several singers, but above all with the famous conductor Hans Richter, with whom he came to be on familiar terms. My father asked Hans Richter, who had written out the fair copy of the score of the *Die Meistersinger*, 'how in fact does one become a conductor?' And Hans Richter answered: 'You get up on the podium — and either you can do it, or else you'll never learn!' That really is true — up to a point. Routine can get you so far, that must be accepted — but to learn conducting is only possible within certain limitations.

My mother also went with my father to the Wagner operas; and when the talk turned to Mozart, it was a case of: 'Mozart, he is totally undramatic with his endless text repetitions.' It was not until several years later that it dawned on me what these 'endless repetitions' should signify.

And so I had come to Munich, to Bruno Walter, who loved Mozart above all else, to the splendid Residenztheater which — sadly not with the same good acoustics — now stands again. It was linked to the National Theatre, and you only had to walk through a passageway to be in the Residenztheater.

I did not miss a single Mozart performance under Bruno Walter and, whenever it was remotely possible, listened in at rehearsals. Bruno Walter noticed my interest, and the unbelievable thing happened: I, the newest and youngest conductor, still in the first year of my engagement at Munich, was allowed to conduct a performance of *Entfü-hrung* with a cast that I should dearly love to have today: Richard Tauber sang Belmonte; Maria Ivogün, Konstanze and Paul Bender, Osmin.

Sadly, Bruno Walter only stayed for one more year in Munich. After him came Knappertsbusch, with whom I had to come to terms, since both externally and inwardly his way of making music was the exact opposite of Bruno Walter's. Also, he was celebrated at that time, when the Nazi movement was getting under way, as the blond, blue-eyed, tall, slim German. I should like to stress, however, that Knappertsbusch was never a Nazi and later had violent quarrels with the regime, finally being removed from Munich by Goebbels. But he was the clear opposite to Bruno Walter, who was a highly sensitive Jew and reminded people somewhat of Gustav Mahler, of whom he often spoke to me, always emphasizing how much he owed to him as his master. Again, I have Bruno Walter to thank for the broadening of my musical horizons. Through Bruno Walter I also got to know Thomas Mann who, by the way, liked me very much from a human and a musical point of view, and whose daughter — I only found out later — I was once supposed to marry.

I should now relate how I met my wife in Munich. She came from a Munich mercantile family and was at the age of sixteen already a pupil of Maria Ivogün. She went for six months to Bamberg and then sang for Bruno Walter, who always took an interest in young singers. He was excited by her and allowed her to make her début on the stage of the National Theatre as Oscar in *Ballo*.

Then I conducted the *Bohème* in which my wife was to sing Mimi, and Bruno Walter kept on saying to me, 'this Thea Linhard has a sweet voice, but it is still very small: of course she is only seventeen. The Puccini orchestra is so terribly loud; keep it down, keep it down!' Thea Linhard became my wife in 1927.

We both suffered from Bruno Walter's departure and were not ashamed to weep at his farewell, but we had to put up with it. Knappertsbusch had little sympathy for my wife, while he got on with me better and better. Later, he treated me on equal terms as a colleague. I gradually advanced and, after a performance of *Der Rosenkavalier*, which I had never conducted before and had to take over at twenty-four hour's notice, I finally won Knappertsbusch's confidence. On that occasion I was lucky that the singers in the third Act did not 'come adrift' — in such an event, someone conducting this opera for the first time is lost. From that point on, Knappertsbusch gave me free rein, above all in Mozart. He himself, as I have to conclude in retrospect, had only a theoretical, abstract relationship with Mozart. I was allowed to conduct *Entführung*, *Figaro* and *Die Zauberflöte*. Then I took over a performance of *Ariadne*, which went very well for me since I had already taken all the rehearsals as *répétiteur* under Oskar Posa.

I wrote a happy letter to my parents about it:

My dear, my good parents! I am happy and must pour out my heart to you. I contrived this conducting of *Ariadne* deliberately to bring about an artistic trial of strength; I came through it brilliantly. Nobody in the orchestra and none of the singers would believe that I was conducting the opera for the first time [and] without rehearsal. At the end Maria Ivogün said to me that she has never sung more easily with anyone, not even Strauss. They all had me brought out and I had to stand *n*-times in front of the curtain amidst the indescribable jubilation of the audience. But I do have to say, without any trace of arrogance, that I acquitted myself brilliantly. According to Schalk the opera is the hardest one to conduct, and moreover a colossal cheek to conduct it without a rehearsal. But I trusted to my artistic powers, and they did not betray me. And without the slightest uncertainty throughout the evening. I would not exchange the feeling of artistic power from last night for a sea of dollars. The orchestra (all the First Professors [senior principals] were playing) gave me a standing ovation as I left the pit, and they all came up to me. What they actually said to me I should really rather not repeat lest I finally get conceited.

And so I passed the test of my first Strauss opera very well. The climax and the end will remain unforgettable for me: I have never heard such a blazing *fff*. It 'exploded,' Mottl would have said. Now I am weeping a quiet tear that you were not there and kiss you a thousand times as your happy

Karl

I was six years in Munich at the National Theatre and during this time, as the Directors informed me on my seventieth birthday, gave about seven hundred opera performances, but as a result was totally out of the running in the concert sector; that remained the preserve of the General Music Director.

I have always involved myself in modern music and so I

made a suggestion for an opera programme in Munich, which, in 1923, was a daring undertaking. I proposed *L'heure espagnole* by Maurice Ravel and *Le Rossignol* by Stravinsky. The orchestral rehearsals used to take place in the foyer of the National Theatre — I do not know whether that is still the case. Portraits of past General Music Directors hung there, and I recall one amusing incident. I went to almost every evening performance and noticed that the musicians always spat as they passed by the bust of General Music Director Herman Zumpe. As this practice continued, I asked: 'Why do you do that?' 'It's been passed on from generation to generation, this spitting,' they said. And then they told me: 'We petitioned the King for a raise in salary, which Zumpe presented for consideration; and he commented: 'I am against the raise; it's better to hunt with hungry hounds!' That came to the ears of the musicians and from then on they spat in front of him.

The foyer is on the main frontage of the theatre, out on the street, opposite the entrance is the Max Joseph monument, with its hand raised in warning: 'Do not enter the National Theatre!' It is on account of that that I can clearly recall one incident. That was Hitler's march into the Feldherrnhalle in 1923. I was once again rehearsing in the foyer *Le Rossignol* by Stravinsky, whose music was later placed on the prohibited list by the Nazis as cultural Bolshevism. Suddenly we heard shots — and indeed, the dead and wounded were brought into the Max Joseph Platz. The government had put out sentries and blockaded public buildings in order to protect them. I had to break off the rehearsal. We were all very anxious, because of course we did not know what was going on outside.

CHAPTER THREE

Darmstadt — All young people, modern,
hard-working and possessed —*Wozzeck* —
Wozzeck in Naples, Buenos Aires, Salzburg, Vienna
and New York — Friendship with Alban Berg —
Schoenberg — The Volkschor in Worms

At the end of 1927 I was offered the post of *Generalmusik-direktor* which had become vacant in Darmstadt. After I had conducted the *Ring, Tristan* and all the 'great' Mozart operas in Munich, I was reluctant to conduct in Darmstadt on a trial basis. They respected that; I presented myself and obtained the post. For my sake, my wife was only singing in concerts at that time. After the war, when Bruno Walter came to Vienna, he invited her for a performance of 'The Seasons' there.

Carl Ebert was at that time the *Generalintendant* in Darmstadt — previously he had been an actor in Frankfurt am Main. Rudolf Bing, the present head of the Metropolitan Opera, was administrative director, and A.M. Rabenalt was the chief producer. We were young people, around thirty years old on average, all with modern views and enormously hard-working. There were great talents in the spoken theatre too, Werner Finck among them.

I started with Handel's *Julius Caesar* in an entirely

modern production by Rabenalt with sets by Wilhelm Reinking, who is now at the Deutsche Oper, Berlin. We created real living, progressive theatre. Then for my official opening performance, I conducted my first *Meistersinger*, with great success. Subsequently I endeavoured to give the first presentation outside Berlin, only a couple of days later, of the most famous works whose premieres Otto Klemperer was conducting in Berlin: *Neues vom Tage* by Hindemith and *Das Leben des Orest* by Křenek for example.

In 1931, when, after three years I had the orchestra and my ensemble firmly in my control, I dared to put on *Wozzeck* by Alban Berg. One should not mistake what a mountain of difficulties accompanied this work in 1931. I have just recorded *Wozzeck* with Dietrich Fischer-Dieskau, and the opera has not become any simpler in the meantime. Then it was more than just hard: I began by rehearsing the individual wind sections on their own, since one often had to give the musicians explanations which took up a good deal of time. The most difficult thing about Alban Berg is his notation, which is, however, part of the essence of the music. One could indeed — and I would pledge myself to do it — rewrite the score, without changing a note or a dynamic marking, in such a way that the opera would be easier to read; but indeed in that case it would not be *Berg*'s *Wozzeck*. In *Lulu*, Berg somewhat reduced the difficulties in the notation — perhaps just a little as a result of my suggestions.

In this context a saying of Richard Strauss's is appropriate: 'The faster I compose the longer I take to write it down.' A classic example of this is the Prelude to the third Act of *Die schweigsame Frau*. If Strauss had written it out in semiquavers it would have been difficult for the musicians to read, in purely visual terms, so he wrote it in semibreves and minims and put a fast metronome mark above it. Alban Berg, by contrast, wrote in semiquavers, and on the last semiquaver the cellos have to play a *pizzicato*, which is hard to read and rhythmically even harder to play, and all the conductor can do is to beat a slow 4/4 and leave it to the players to divide up the beats for themselves, as had been worked through in rehearsal. For this *Wozzeck* we had about thirty-four rehearsals!

And now I should like to come to my meeting with Alban Berg, which was such a happy one, and say — not least out of gratitude to its creator — that after the war, I helped *Wozzeck* towards its international success. Then, after its première in Salzburg, with Willi Schuh as producer, this opera conquered the whole world.

I have conducted *Wozzeck* everywhere, even in Italian with Tito Gobbi in the Teatro San Carlo in Naples, where the Director kept his theatre closed for a whole month, and once again I scheduled thirty-four orchestral rehearsals. Up to the eighteenth rehearsal I could see no light at the end of the tunnel. I rehearsed — it worked. I rehearsed again — it didn't work. The Neapolitans are really good folk. The musicians were badly paid but the dearest creatures — there is just one thing they do have, however: a love of talking which is unstoppable. And of course, they talk in the rehearsals. Consequently I often stopped conducting and said: '*Io ho tempo*'. ('I've got time.') And then they had to stay behind. But I only discovered this solution later — at the beginning I did not have that much patience and behaved like my Italian colleagues letting loose furious screams. That did not bother them in the least, for they were used to it. I remember the passacaglia in the first Act in the scene with Wozzeck and the Doctor; there is a passage for the cellos which is very difficult rhythmically, and since the orchestra members were always talking, it never worked. So I flung down the baton and simply went away. Then they all came running after me shouting: '*Maestro, ritorna per favore!*' ['Maestro, please come back!']

When I returned, something happened that I shall never forget: the musicians stood up and passed to me Dolce and vermouth on a tray — and then the orchestra struck up *O sole mio*. And how passionately those Neapolitans played it!

Wozzeck had such a response in Naples that it had to be repeated the following year. Gobbi, who interpreted the role, especially in the third Act, in neoveristic style, was an outstanding performer of the title role, and as an actor, too.

I also put on a performance of *Wozzeck* in the Teatro Colón in Buenos Aires. The German text was translated into Spanish for the audience, and as a result other works by Georg Büchner, *Dantons Tod*, for example, were also translated into Spanish. Last but not least, I beavered away for years until I was able to conduct the work at the Metropolitan Opera, and the public's reception was so good that it had to be repeated the following year there, too. And finally, I chose *Wozzeck* as the first opera to be staged in the rebuilt Vienna State Opera.

Alban Berg came to Darmstadt about eight or ten days before the first performance there. I had no idea whether I had got it right, despite Berg's precise metronome markings; but after the first words he exchanged with me, I lost any trace of nervousness. He and his wife were for me the most ideal, the finest and dearest people, the kindest that I have ever got to know.

The Viennese première under Clemens Krauss had taken place before my Darmstadt performances; but Alban Berg still said to me, 'despite the magnificent Philharmonic, I prefer this performance.' And we remained friends until his all-too-early death. Alban Berg wrote in my copy of the *Wozzeck* score: 'The Darmstadt *Wozzeck* on 28 February 1931 was for me a great and happy occasion, not only because it was a wonderful success, but because it brought me into contact for the first time with an especially dear man and splendid musician, Dr Karl Böhm. A thousand thanks from his Alban Berg.'

I met him now and then on holiday, first at Lake Ossiach and later at the Wörthersee. There I was one of the first to whom he showed the first Act of his *Lulu* score. He explained to me why he had written this part for a coloratura soprano. He wanted to show the coldness of a woman who does not know why she is so attractive to men, not just the slut, as one often sees her on the stage. I was very proud to have brought this opera to Vienna a few years ago, to the Theater an der Wien, and also to have been the first to conduct it, in 1968, in Berlin, where the first performance of *Wozzeck* had taken place.

Through Alban Berg and his wife, who is still a friend of mine, I came to know and love the whole Mahler circle, and, from their stories, Alban Berg's teacher Arnold Schoenberg and his friend Anton von Webern. I can still remember clearly how one day Berg, when I could not praise *Wozzeck* highly enough, said to me: 'I am a nothing alongside Schoenberg.' And I answered: 'Don't be cross with me but the second part of Schoen*berg* is dearer to me than the whole.' I meant nothing against Schoenberg by that, from whom, indeed, the whole twelve-tone system originates and who, if only for that reason, became one of the Greats of music — but Schoenberg was really not in his element as a stage dramatist, while Berg's genius as a dramatist could be seen even in his choice of materials. While studying *Lulu* — and, above all, *Wozzeck* — one is aware of how enormously gifted Berg was; able to subordinate the strictest forms, such as passacaglia, fugue and variation, to the dramatic action in such a way that the listener does not even become conscious of it. I remember that Berg himself used to give lectures about *Wozzeck* and would say to the audience at the end 'and now, forget everything that I have said, and just let the drama work on you!'

Other new works I performed in Darmstadt during that period were *Die schwarze Kammer* by Ernst Roters, *Judith* by Honegger, *Valerio* (after *Leonce und Lena*) by the Darmstadt composer Hans Simon, then *Sly* by Ermano Wolf-Ferrari and *Jonny spielt auf* by Křenek.

My contract in Darmstadt was from 1927 to 1933. In 1928, on 16 March our only son, Karlheinz, came into the world. At the end of 1930 I conducted a performance there of *Die Meistersinger* which was attended by Leopold Sachse, the Intendant of Hamburg. Sachse was so enthused that he asked me to succeed Egon Pollak, who was then going to Chicago. I had great difficulty in getting released from Darmstadt, but eventually they allowed me to go. The saddest one of all was Ebert, who said to me: 'Now you're leaving me here all alone in this dump', which is what Darmstadt was, really, apart from the theatre. A few months later, however, Ebert got the job of Intendant of the City Opera in Berlin; he went there together with Rudolf Bing.

In Darmstadt I also conducted all the symphony concerts and, in the course of these four years, conducted principally the entire classical repertoire, but with a new work in almost every concert. Alongside my eight regular symphony concerts, each with a formal public rehearsal, I also conducted the Darmstadt Singverein, with which I performed almost all of the great choral works. The chorus was willing, but not so outstanding vocally, since it was on the elderly side. Then I received a commission from Bürgermeister Rahn of Worms — he was an upright man who had successfully stood up to the Nazis. Of course he was dismissed from his post and interned, but later released.

Bürgermeister Rahn invited me to conduct a newly-founded amateur choir — and what did I choose as the first piece? Verdi's *Requiem*. This choir was still completely untrained vocally when I arrived for the first rehearsal. Bürgermeister Rahn himself sang with them, and next to him a fitter or a stonemason. The members of the choir were chosen without regard to their occupation. Only their voices counted. And the vocal material was really good, completely unformed, real Rhenish voices. I had the great joy — if only after many, many rehearsals, for the choir had first to be taught the basic principles of singing — to achieve a very nice performance.

There were about that time two especially good years for wine, 1921 and 1925. In gratitude the Bürgermeister presented me with five bottles of Liebfrauenmilch from each of these two years. I know the vineyard near the Liebfrauenkirche in Worms where these grapes grow, and I cannot help laughing when I think of this ridiculously small patch of earth and see how much 'Liebfrauenmilch'* is drunk in America alone!

With this choir I later performed Brahms' *Deutsches Requiem*, and got a lot of pleasure from its musical development. I remained in touch with Bürgermeister Rahn, he answered a letter from me just the day before he died. He was then eighty-five years old, and his daughter told me later that my letter had been his final pleasure.

* German wine labelling laws are more strict than the author implies: the mass market brand using grapes other than from this specific vineyard is in fact marketed as *Liebfraumilch*, a subtle but adequate distinction! (Tr)

CHAPTER FOUR

Hamburg — The musical party — *Tristan* in Vienna —
The first Philharmonic concert in Vienna —
Forest scents — Dresden —
The departure of Fritz Busch — An ensemble —
The Sächsische Staatskapelle — Tour to London —
Bruckner — The original versions

There are cities in which you only have to walk through the door of the theatre to have an instantaneous success; in other cities you only get hard knocks no matter how hard you try. One city where it went well from the start was Hamburg. Hamburg loves me today as much as it did then, as was shown by the last concert there with the Vienna Philharmonic, and that love has remained mutual.

Right from my very first appearance I was greeted by the Hamburg public with open arms. Hamburgers are linked to the whole world by the sea, and are open to everything. They are neither narrow-minded nor cold. On the contrary: I know of no more warm-hearted public.

In Hamburg I came into contact with Richard Strauss for the first time, albeit briefly. I should like to take this opportunity to say that I firmly believe that people who have something to communicate usually, or almost always, have the good fortune to get the right help at the right time.

So it was with my teacher Weiss in Graz, later with Mandyczewski, then came the fateful meeting with Bruno Walter, to whom I owe the overcoming of my egotism, for if, as everyone says, I had not done the right thing then, looking back now, I should have remained in Graz, and everything that was important and positive in my development would not have happened. It was just the same with my meeting with the genius Richard Strauss, despite all the reservations held against him, be they personal, political and now, sometimes, even artistic. . .

In Hamburg some time during 1932 — the events of 1933 were already looming — I was asked by a Hamburg lawyer to meet him. I thought it was something to do with the Opera — but it turned out to be something quite different. He came to me and informed me that the Nazi party were going to appoint him *Reichsleiter* of Hamburg. I was, of course, an Aryan, he said, and Leopold Sachse would naturally have to disappear, and he would offer me the post of *Generalintendant* of the Hamburg State Opera in his place. Was I not a member of the (then) illegal NSDAP? I informed him that I was not a member of his party. 'Then you'll have to join,' he said, to which I rejoined that I was already a member of a party and was therefore unable to do so. So he asked me: 'What are you? German Nationalist? Christian Socialist?' 'No.' 'Are you a Communist?' 'No.' 'Are you a Socialist?' 'No.' 'Not that either . . . What the hell are you then?' 'I belong to only *one* party: the musical party.' And then, as he was about to say something: 'I'm quite serious. I have never been a member of a party, not even a Volunteer Fire Brigade, and I never shall join one. Even at the university I was never in a student guild. I concern myself only with music.' That has been my position to the present day, incidentally. So, of course, I did not become *Generalintendant* in Hamburg, but despite that I was invited to go to the prestigious opera house in Dresden.

The Hamburg opera management consented to my going. I was on very friendly terms with Egon Pollak; he was married to a lady from Graz and had lived in Isestrasse, right next door to us. So that it should not be suspected that I had driven him from his post, I arranged a guest contract for him which kept him linked to Hamburg in so far as his American commitments permitted. He conducted the *Ring* each year and was a phenomenal musician. Later he went to Prague where he died suddenly in tragic circumstances. He had a weak heart and had had severe inflammation of the lungs: during a performance of *Fidelio*, at '*Mir ist so wunderbar*' ('It is so wondrous') he dropped the baton, was just able to leave the podium and died backstage.

It was during this time in Hamburg that I conducted *Elektra* for the first time. I had already conducted *Salome* in Darmstadt. There was also a new production of *Arabella*.

Sachse himself did most of the productions. He was a cautious, experienced practitioner of stagecraft, who rejected modernism — and compared to Darmstadt, Hamburg seemed old-fashioned to me. Sachse was no longer a young man then; he soon had to emigrate to New York on political grounds and became a teacher and producer there.

It was then that I conducted *Das Herz* by Hans Pfitzner and *Die Soldaten* by Manfred Gurlitt, the latter a dreadful performance and a dreadful piece. It was, indeed, the last performance of mine that my father heard. He knew of my invitation to Dresden, but he saw none of my performances there.

It was on the occasion of *Arabella* that I wrote to Richard Strauss. It was about cuts, which he always resisted. He said then, and ever since: 'If I'd wanted it different, I wouldn't have written that! You ought not to ask!'

While I was still at Hamburg the first feelers came in my direction from Dresden. In the meantime, however, an

invitation came to conduct *Tristan und Isolde* at the Vienna
State Opera. From what has gone before one can readily
gauge what this invitation meant, since for me the name of
this institution was bound up with my conception of the
highest operatic art. The young man who had sat in the
gods of that august theatre from 1910 to 1918 was suddenly
to stand on the same podium where Gustav Mahler and
Bruno Walter had performed, where Franz Schalk was still
performing. Naturally I accepted the invitation. I had just
one orchestra rehearsal, but got on very well with the
members of the Philharmonic,* whom I was meeting on
this occasion for the first time. The next day's performance
was a really great success.

I have a lively recollection of a man, whom one can say I
practically worshipped as a student and for whose sake I
went to every *Parsifal*: Richard Mayr. He sang King Mark.
The evening before the performance Hugo Burghauser, the
Chairman of the Philharmonic, came to me and invited me
to conduct a Vienna Philharmonic concert. This took place
in April that same year, 1933. There are some snapshots of
one of the rehearsals, and I have so often looked at the old
face of a Rosé, a Buxbaum and a Wunderer. The programme of the concert: the *Haffner* Symphony by Mozart,

---

* The orchestra which plays in the Vienna State Opera is correctly
designated the 'Vienna State Opera Orchestra', (*Wiener Staatsopernor-
chester*) whose members are salaried employees, under the management
of the Opera, and effectively, civil servants. The Vienna Philharmonic
Orchestra, (*Wiener Philharmoniker*) is the independent, self-governing
concert orchestra drawn from the members of the Opera orchestra: when
the 'first team' is in the pit in the Opera, this is virtually identical to the
Vienna Philharmonic. Aspirant members of the Philharmonic may
spend some time in the Opera orchestra before being admitted as full
members of the Philharmonic. Since the orchestra principals are generally also professors at the Vienna Conservatoire, new members of the
Philharmonic are still often recruited from among their students, a
tradition which contributes to the preservation of the Orchestra's style.
(Tr)

Brahms' Second Symphony, and Beethoven's Fifth. I compiled this programme at Hugo Burghauser's request, for since then I have never conducted two such standard works as the Brahms and Beethoven symphonies one after the other in a concert. Incidentally, after the *Tristan* I was even asked, through intermediaries, whether I should like to take over the Vienna State Opera. Since this happened behind the back of Clemens Krauss, who was absent at the time, I refused.

Straight after the Vienna *Tristan* I drove to Dresden and at the beginning of May conducted another *Tristan* there. As soon as the first Act was over they offered me the post of Opera Director which was left void following the ugly departure of Fritz Busch. I was still contracted to Hamburg, however, and so was not able to accept immediately. The theatre in Dresden, the acoustics and the Sächsische Staatskapelle had made such an impression on me, however, that I flirted with the idea of accepting this post, if Hamburg would grant me an early release from my contract.

Incidentally, I overheard a conversation between two orchestral players from the Sächsische Staatskapelle who were talking about me without being aware that I was there. One of them said, in broad Saxon, 'At least we won't have to make allowances for the dialect — we know that already!' — for one of my famous predecessors, Ernst von Schuch, was from Graz, like me.

I went back to Hamburg and asked for an early release, especially since Leopold Sachse, whom I so revered, had in the meantime had to leave his post, and Heinrich Strohm had come to Hamburg as his successor. I did *Der Freischütz* in Hamburg with him. I went in to the dress rehearsal and saw that, in an otherwise totally modern production, he had put real pine trees on the stage. By the end of the third performance there were only sticks left. And, I thought, can that be right, can I really smell pine needles? Strohm had sprayed pine scent around the place so that as you entered, you noticed that in *Der Freischültz* it smelt of a German forest. A year later I received the release I had requested and took up my post in Dresden in January 1934.

During a performance of *Rigoletto* — it was all rigged — Fritz Busch was whistled at by a few Nazis, and another conductor in the Dresden State Opera was standing by in his tails to take over the performance of the opera. I want to say something about this occurrence, because it was said later that I drove Busch out of his post. I spent a lot of time with him in Vienna, and he knew very well that I had nothing to do with it, since I had not set foot in Dresden until just four months before his departure. Following this scandal, although he was an 'Aryan', Fritz Busch voluntarily emigrated.

Later, it was equally held against me that I did not emigrate. People from abroad also asked questions on this subject, to which it remained to me only to reply: at that time I had no invitations from the Met or from Covent Garden. On account of my family I could not give up a secure position except in the most extreme circumstances, but I believe, in the course of my work in Dresden, as in Vienna later, I had always proved on which side I stood.

After the departure of Fritz Busch from Dresden, Kutzschbach took over the provisional direction of the Dresden State Opera: he remained Opera Director for some while, but only on paper, since I had full authority as Director right from the start. My first performance took place on January 7, 1934: once again with *Die Meistersinger*.

That period in Dresden was perhaps artistically my most fruitful, since, although the political situation was anything but pleasant and later, with the outbreak of war, became extremely precarious, I had the possibility of carrying out artistically something I was never able to do later. That is,

really to build an ensemble which was at my constant
disposal for rehearsals, thus enabling me to prepare the
most difficult of ensemble operas, to perform them four or
five times, to revive them once more with the same cast and
then to experience a performance which went like a premiere after just a single short rehearsal. Apart from that,
the individual orchestra parts were always taken by the
same musicians, despite the fact that the Orchestra of the
Dresden State Opera was a hundred strong, so that
changes would certainly have been possible. For artistic
reasons, once the personnel for an opera was fixed, it
remained in force for every subsequent performance.

All in all I conducted six hundred and eighty-nine
performances, which makes about a hundred opera performances per year. As well as these there were the subscription concerts, ten in a year, in each case a public rehearsal
in the morning and the performance in the evening. These
concerts were given from the stage, which was not the
happiest solution; but the theatre had such magnificent
acoustics that close contact with the audience was always
maintained.

I only once refused to conduct the public rehearsal on
the same day as the concert, and that was for a work which
I held was impossible to experience twice in one day as it
should be experienced; Beethoven's 'Ninth'. I started the
custom — Wagner was the first to do this — of playing this
work on Palm Sunday every year, but with the public
rehearsal as an evening concert the preceding Saturday. I
kept up this tradition and in Dresden alone conducted the
'Ninth' twenty times, fourteen of them with Maria Cebotari
in the soprano part.

I also tried to include a new work in every programme. I
did not allow myself to be deflected from this, either
because I was one hundred percent convinced by the work
or by the feeling that here was a development which had to

be shown to the audience, or simply because, when the new Messiah of music for whom we are always waiting comes along, he will not be remotely understood and he will have enough problems already.

In this Strauss theatre my first new production was, of course, a Richard Strauss opera, *Der Rosenkavalier*. I had scheduled seventeen orchestral rehearsals for this production — despite the fact that the orchestra in Dresden had already played this opera a hundred and ninety-nine times. Ernst von Schuch conducted the first performance, Richard Strauss himself conducted the hundredth, I the two hundredth. The orchestral rehearsals for this performance were extremely productive, and I was able to correct some fourteen or fifteen serious mistakes in the parts. After the final rehearsal, Konzertmeister Jan Damen — he was a Dutchman and later became leader of the Amsterdam Concertgebouw Orchestra — said, 'not a single rehearsal was too much, this opera has not grown any easier technically.'

At the première of this *Rosenkavalier* the three ladies who sang the Terzetto in the very first performance were in the auditorium, and Richard Strauss declared later: 'I have to say that this Terzett is at least the equal of that in the first performance.' The new cast was: Martha Fuchs, singing the part of Marschallin for the first time, Maria Cebotari (Sophie) and Tiana Lemnitz (Octavian).

Then I did Handel's *Julius Caesar*, a new work for Dresden, and later the world première of *Der Günstling* by Wagner-Régeny. Now that really was a work that one could — indeed should — put on the agenda. The piece, to a text by Caspar Neher, was cast in a style quite different from any works being written at that time: in an almost modern Handelian style, I should say, with the most modest orchestral resources and yet compellingly dramatic. Then came the première of *Die schweigsame Frau* with Friedrich

Plaschke 'the Indestructible' as Strauss wrote, and Maria
Cebotari in the principal roles, then *Der verlorene Sohn* by
Robert Heger, *Massimilia Doni* by Othmar Schoeck, the first
performance of the ballet *Jeux de cartes* by Stravinsky, the
Die Wirtin von Pinsk by Richard Mohaupt, a dramatically
very effective opera with an excellent text which then had
but one flaw: the wife of the composer was a 'non-Aryan'.
After the fourth performance I had a guest engagement in
Florence and while I was away, the regional governor
forbade any further performances.

There followed the performance of the Strauss opera
dedicated to me, *Daphne*, and finally a work by Heinrich
Sutermeister, who had meanwhile became very well
known. *Romeo und Julia* was the first effort by this composer,
and this time it was not true what Decsey once wrote in a
review — 'first operas and puppies should be drowned,' —
for it remained Sutermeister's best work. Maria Cebotari
sang Julia on that occasion. Later came the première of
Monteverdi's *Orfeo* in the arrangement by Orff, together
with Orff's *Carmina Burana*. And then a final première —
the ninth in my Dresden time: *Die Zauberinsel*, also by
Sutermeister, after Shakespeare's 'Tempest'. This was,
however, a long way from having the importance of *Romeo
und Julia* for the simple reason that Sutermeister wanted to
write an attractive work that would be thoroughly effective
with an audience, which is something one ought not do. To
write with an eye to public success never does any good. He
wanted to write a massive C major finale in the style of
Richard Strauss (*Friedenstag*) right at the end of the opera.
It takes a Beethoven to achieve such a finale, elevating the
music into timeless, eternal regions, as indeed he succeeded
in doing in *Fidelio*.

During my time in Dresden I personally prepared all of
Wagner (scenically as well as musically), all the 'great'
Mozarts — almost the entire Richard Strauss, almost the

entire Verdi, among them an opera which has only today come to be recognized; *Macbeth*.

And since I have come to 'singers' opera', I had in Dresden a dazzling international ensemble of singers. I shall just mention the names: Maria Cebotari, Martha Fuchs, who was originally a mezzo-soprano then changed to the dramatic *Fach* and later sang a splendid Brünnhilde and Isolde (but only for a short time, as I prophesied, for her voice was not able to sustain the soprano register for long). She was such a full-blooded singer that she said to me, 'God, I'm so bored by these mezzo-soprano roles, I simply must sing Brünnhilde and Isolde even if I can only do it for ten years.' I brought Margarete Teschemacher from Stuttgart: she was Daphne to perfection and, above all, unbeatable in the Italian soprano roles. Martha Rohs was there, Elisabeth Höngen and Christel Goltz, whom I later took to Vienna, then Erna Sack. In the baritone and bass *Fach* there was Josef Herrmann, Mathieu Ahlers-meyer, Kurt Böhme and Sven Nilsson, a Swedish bass, and Paul Schöffler whom I also, to my great joy, met again in Vienna. There was Torsten Ralf, a splendid Swedish tenor, and 'last but not least' Friedrich Plaschke, whom I have already mentioned. He was over sixty when I took up my appointment and sang Hans Sachs with me about fifty times mastering the part without the slightest sign of tiredness. He was married to the famous dramatic soprano Eva von der Osten, the first Octavian, who was the producer of *Arabella* in my time, but who no longer performed on stage.

In Dresden I had all the rights and duties of Opera Director. I had to deal with financial matters, but had a generously-staffed administration within which and above all, apart from the Intendant, there was an excellent administrative director. He was the son of the famous conductor Ernst von Schuch, Dr Friedrich von Schuch, with whom I remained in touch to the end of his life — he was then living in retirement in Munich. After Hamburg, where Sachse gave me a very free hand, I fully took up the responsibility for planning the repertoire and for the choice of singers. As I hope I have shown by the names I have mentioned, I believe that I assembled a truly international ensemble of singers. This duty was made easier by the fact that singers in those days were able only to travel little or not at all, and once war broke out, it was quite impossible for them to travel, with the exception of little domestic tours.

Our guest appearance of the Dresden State Opera at Covent Garden in London in 1936 proved how well prepared this ensemble was. Unlike today, London did not have an opera ensemble and, through our performances, it saw for the first time what can be achieved with a permanent ensemble. I can still recall it exactly: Strauss attended the performance in the stage box. I conducted *Der Rosenkavalier* with the cast I have already mentioned, and the applause after the first Act lasted over twenty minutes, filling the scene shift from the first to the second Act. Londoners formed long queues for tickets, and I myself saw how patiently they waited through the night and the following day in order to get hold of tickets for a performance. In London we gave *Rosenkavalier, Tristan, Don Giovanni, Figaro*. I conducted all of these operas myself, Richard Strauss conducted his *Ariadne*.

Then there were two concerts in the Queen's Hall, one of which was conducted by Richard Strauss and the other by me. I then had the courage — and this courage was rewarded — to conduct a thoroughly unpopular programme, namely with Bruckner's Fourth (in the original version moreover) as the last work. In this version the symphony lasted over an hour and the audience listened with such attention, and the applause was so frenetic that I had to add the *Meistersinger* prelude as an encore.

As a Wagnerian I had a profound relationship with Bruckner. I had already conducted several of his symphonies in Darmstadt, but especially in Dresden, where a Bruckner Association and a Bruckner Society were established, I had stood up for Bruckner in almost every concert series. From this Society, of which I was a member, I later received the Gold Medal of Honour.

In London I got my first offer from a record company, the Electrola Company, which is called 'His Master's Voice' in England. For this Company the main works I conducted were Bruckner's Fourth and Fifth in the original version which had been published by the Viennese Professor Josef Haas together with Else Krüger. It was, of course, a risk recording the original versions of Bruckner; the version usually played then included major cuts. To put a symphony on record without cuts on the old discs — there weren't such things as long-playing records — meant that you could only play for four to five minutes and a few seconds and then find a break. That was far from easy.

I have performed Bruckner again and again, all the symphonies, and I am absolutely convinced that one must play the original versions. I have compared the texts, now revised by Professor Leopold Nowak, and established that the latest editions correspond to the desires and the wishes of Bruckner.

Franz Schalk, later the Director of the Vienna State Opera and his brother Josef, who performed such services for Bruckner's works, certainly had the best of intentions when they argued for cuts, since they believed that in this way they would be able to bring the work of Bruckner to a broader public. This assumption, as it later turned out, however, is wrong, for either one has a point of contact or else one never will have. On the contrary, I have often noticed with Wagner that with cuts the masterpieces lose their structure and become disjointed. After all, the great composers were indeed masters of form.

The Schalk brothers also made changes in the instrumentation and added some elements of Wagnerian orchestration, despite the fact that Bruckner, although he sounds similar to Wagner in certain combinations of chords, actually prefers a different form of orchestration. For Bruckner comes from the organ, and that is how he orchestrates. Out of deep conviction, and not only as an Austrian, I have promoted Bruckner in other countries, and have established it as a fact that, where there is an orchestra convinced to a man by his music, it never fails to make its effect. I have recently seen this on my tour with the Vienna Philharmonic in the United States. Everybody advised me against touring America with Bruckner's Eighth as the main work on the programme. I was stubborn and told myself, 'you're sure to have a success with this work with an orchestra like the Vienna Philharmonic, who have it, as it were, in their blood.'

And so it turned out: in New York or in Raleigh, North Carolina, where we had audiences of ten to eleven thousand for each concert. There were two concerts there. We wanted to change the programme, but were asked to play the same programme on both evenings, as there were more people. We played the great G minor Symphony by Mozart and Bruckner's Eighth, and I had the joy of seeing that nobody left the hall, but on the contrary the audience applauded enthusiastically at the end. But I am certain that without my colleagues' preparation, principally the emigrés, who have indeed taken over most of the cultural education, such a success in a town like Raleigh would not have been possible. In New York, where I played Bruckner's Fourth and Seventh, I had the pleasure of a member of the New York Philharmonic saying to me, 'what a pity it's all over.'

As I have said: the attitude of an orchestra to such a solitary and unique phenomenon as Bruckner is decisive; for if we on the platform are all convinced, then we shall be able to convince our audience!

CHAPTER FIVE

First Directorship in Vienna —
The Viennese Mozart Style — A torn-up letter —
Visit to Switzerland — Theatres closed —
Wartime confusion in Berlin —
The Vienna Philharmonic

The first feelers in my direction from Vienna came as early as 1941. From a credible source I learned, however, that the 'Lord on High' was opposed to my appointment at that time. The fact that I had not joined the Nazi party may have had something to do with it as well as the whole business of *Die schweigsame Frau*. Ernst August Schneider had temporarily taken over the State Opera, in which the current government Cultural Adviser, Walter Thomas, took a close interest. Despite opposition from Berlin, Thomas forced through my appointment and via political channels obtained my release from my still-current Dresden contract. During my period of activity in Dresden I had in any case been conducting more and more in Vienna, both in the State Opera and the Konzerthaus, where I had led my own concert series as the head of the Vienna Symphony Orchestra.

As Opera Director in Vienna I naturally wanted to give of my best. I found there a really good complement of singers which I completed, as I have said, with numerous principal singers from my Dresden ensemble. But it was already 1944 and little did I know that I should be granted scarcely one year as Director, since in 1944 the total closure of the theatres was promulgated.

I began with a new production of *Die Meistersinger*. Then we put on a Verdi week. I opened it with *Macbeth*, with Elisabeth Höngen as Lady Macbeth. I wrote about her in my journal: 'The greatest tragedienne in the world!' Schöffler was a magnificent Macbeth. Hans Hotter sang Macbeth in the second performance. During this Verdi week I also conducted *Aïda*, *Ballo* and *Otello*.

The *Ballo* was a new production for Vienna, with wonderful sets by Caspar Neher in a production by Oscar Fritz Schuh. Also by Neher and Schuh was an unforgettable new production of *Otello*, with Lorenz, who sang and acted the title role thrillingly. He was so inspired and had got inside the role to such an extent that he even went to Willy Forst's film studio before the première to have his make-up done by Forst himself. Maria Reining sang a wonderful Desdemona, with Ahlersmayer as Iago.

In the meantime, at the request of the Sächsische Staatskapelle, I conducted my last Dresden 'Ninth', at Easter, April 17 and 18, 1943.

Among my finest memories from that time in Vienna remains the Mozart performance in the Vienna Redoutensaal, regarded, especially abroad, as exemplary. I have particularly lively recollections of *Figaro* and *Così* in Oscar Fritz Schuh's production with sets by Caspar Neher. The solutions which these artists found are quite different from those to which Rennert has come today. If one can speak of a modern realism with Günther Rennert, the performances then were stylized. In the production Schuh had taken great care scenically to create a musical structure just as Mozart had done in purely musical terms.

We had splendid singers at our disposal. Irmgard Seefried was Fiordiligi; Martha Rohs was Dorabella; Anton Dermota, Fernando; Erich Kunz, Guglielmo; and Paul Schöffler, unforgettable as the philosopher Alfonso. In *Figaro*, Schöffler and Kunz alternated as the Count. A French newspaper wrote about *Così* in 1944 — and one can imagine that the French did not have much good to say about us at that time — that this performance would have deserved to have been preserved on film for all time.

These Viennese performances of *Figaro* and *Così* had the great advantage of the same cast being always at my disposal. I would rather cancel a performance than risk having a guest artist endanger such well-established productions. In that way I was able to maintain the standard of these performances right up to the end of my time in Vienna.

I have already mentioned that Bruno Walter impelled me towards my passion for Mozart. If it were possible for it to be increased, then that was something I experienced through Richard Strauss, who opened up to me the last mysteries of, in my view, the greatest of musical geniuses.

My final Vienna premières before the theatres were closed were *Capriccio*, which I then also conducted in Zurich, and *Carmen*. In 1943 I was invited to conduct *Tristan* at the June Festival in the Zurich City Theatre.

We had earlier taken our son, with medical certificates confirming a certain weakness of the lungs, to the Lyceum Alpinum in Zuoz where we could keep him away from all of the wartime and post-war events. As things were to turn out, this was of the greatest importance for my son's development, although it was an emotional burden for us, since at the end of the war we had no news of each other for months on end. After the occupation of Vienna, Käthe Dorsch put us up in a room on the Attersee where Max Lorenz and his wife had also been accommodated. We had a room above the chicken shed which was only unpleasant in so far as we were always woken by the chickens early in the morning. One remarkable thing occurred during our stay in that room: once, when I went for a walk with my wife, I found a torn scrap of paper. I immediately recognized my wife's handwriting — it was a piece of a letter which she had posted to Zuoz from Vienna — and here it lay in the grass at the Attersee. I found other pieces of paper, and we were able to reassemble practically the entire letter. How that letter got there, a letter from Vienna to my son in Switzerland, I cannot explain to this day.

I welcomed the guest appearance with *Capriccio* in the Zurich City Theatre in the June Festival of 1944 not least because it presented an opportunity to earn Swiss francs, which I so badly needed for our son's upkeep. Then three men took a hand: Wilhelm Backhaus, who had meanwhile become a Swiss citizen and was living in Lugano; Gustav Hussnigg, who had gone to elementary school with me and had made a considerable fortune with his discoveries; and the Strauss biographer Dr Willi Schuh — all fanatical opponents of the Nazi regime. They all got together and paid all the necessary expenses for our son Karlheinz up to and beyond the end of the war. They went even further: as we parted at the railway station in Zurich — both they and we knew into what an inferno we were going — they offered, should we wish to stay there, to take care of our living costs until I was once again in a position to earn. When I timidly enquired about that in Vienna, I got the reply: 'Yes, you have an elderly mother and two brothers in Graz, we'll hold on to them.' Then I learned that the law providing for the imprisonment of next-of-kin had come into effect, and I could not square it with my conscience to deliver up my mother and brothers to the Nazis. It was August 2. Soon after that came the closure of the theatres and the declaration of 'total war' which Goebbels so 'grandly' staged with his speech in the Sportpalast in Berlin.

Nevertheless I did all I could in Vienna to save my people from being called up for military service or into the armaments industry. I put on concert performances of operatic excerpts. And there I recall one of my most unforgettable experiences. Before the first programme I asked myself what would be the best thing to perform in such a pinchbeck programme. It was sure to work, a concert performance of the first Act of *Die Walküre* with its ecstatic melodies and the end of the third Act, the Brünnhilde-Wotan duet with the Magic Fire Music. Max Lorenz, in his prime, sang Siegmund, and I remember that I could hardly stop myself laughing as he sang '*Ein Schwert verhiess mir der Vater*' in evening dress. I realized that this scene, indeed the whole Act, is conceived so purely in terms of the theatre that it was quite impossible to lift it away from the stage. On the other hand, when, three or four days later, I performed fragments of *Figaro* and *Così fan tutte*, I came to recognize that in Mozart one can achieve the same effect without a theatre. His music is timeless, whether it be theatre or concert music.

During my Vienna years, in addition to the Vienna Philharmonic, I still conducted the Berlin Philharmonic, with whom I remained in constant contact from 1934. I can bring to mind one concert in 1944 which is not one of the most pleasant memories of my life. At that time there were constant bombing raids on Berlin, and the good folk of the Philharmonic had, with the best of intentions, put me up in Potsdam. Just then the first serial bombing raids on Potsdam started. During the night — my wife had fortunately given me some candles — the light went out and I had to go into the air raid shelter where there were only women, children and empty wine bottles. The shelter was not very deep and would have afforded little protection against a direct hit.

The next day I conducted a concert in a cinema. I had put on some light clothing, thinking that the place would be heated. The concert took place in the morning, because the raids started in the afternoons. The Philharmonic was sitting there in hats and coats: it was cold, zero degrees at the most. I conducted a Haydn symphony for which I otherwise use only very sparing gestures. For this performance I moved more than I do for my morning exercises, just to get warm. Since nothing was any use, I went to my room and changed during the interval. Then I conducted Beethoven's Seventh in long-johns and two pullovers, with the maximum of movement but still could not work up a sweat. And then, to cap it all — off went the sirens. I wanted to go back to Vienna that night and already had a sleeping compartment. It was a heavy air attack, the Royal Palace was in flames, the Berlin State Opera was hit once again, and the man at the station barrier said: 'You cannot travel. All the rails are smashed. There aren't any more trains.' So I stayed put.

A helpful man, a friend of the Philharmonic and a great art lover, took pity on me and invited me to spend the night with him right outside Berlin. We did not get to his house until about midnight and went on to discuss the terrible political situation. In the morning I hurried to the airport where a military plane took me aboard, because I said that I had to conduct in Vienna that same night. It was miserably cold. The people had to sit on a steel rail, as there were no seats. Then a Berliner said to me: 'Would you care for a cognac?' I declined: 'I can't take cognac.' He replied, 'which would you rather have, a solid hangover or a solid lung infection?' The two of us then drank a whole bottle of cognac, and I arrived in Vienna more than a mite tipsy.

This is where the concert performances of opera and opera recordings for the radio took place. The tapes were put in store during the post-war negotiations and then disappeared without trace, but, lo and behold, they turned up again on American records — *Macbeth, Otello* and *Carmen.*

We played factory concerts with the Vienna Philharmonic for Siemens-Schukert and others. For the Philharmonic concert series the principal conductors were Clemens Krauss and Wilhelm Furtwängler.

When today, by unanimous vote of the Vienna Philharmonic on the occasion of their 120th anniversary I was elected Honorary Conductor (a title which had not existed up to then), after I had earlier received the Nicolai Medal, the Ring of Honour and Honorary Membership, and when I look back on my relationship with this association of artists, these are the first uneradicable impressions that I received during my at first sporadic — later permanent — visits to Vienna both in the concert hall and in the Opera.

While still a student in 1913/1914 I heard all of the Philharmonic concerts and I remember a Beethoven cycle which Weingartner conducted, where really all of the qualities of the Orchestra appeared before me at their most highly cultivated. This orchestra is simply unsurpassed in its homogeneity and versatility, and above all its characteristic ability, unique anywhere in the world, of being magnificent in concert as well as opera performances. And not only that. It is also unique in that it is an orchestra which governs itself and was able to preserve this independent administration throughout the Nazi period and all the turbulence of the post-war years. This independent administration means not only that the Orchestra governs itself, but also elects its management, in a secret, democratic vote. Only conductors who have gained a majority of the votes in a secret ballot may conduct Philharmonic concerts. That has the advantage that in its concerts the Orchestra comprises the most strictly selected musicians, while in the Opera, sadly, this strict selection does not always take place, since the musicians there are subordinate to the Opera management.

The characteristic of this Orchestra is, as I have said, its perfect homogeneity; that is to say, the musicians share the same accent not only in their speech (there are practically only Viennese in the Orchestra) but musically too. This comes about through the principal winds and strings and so on also being teachers at the Academy, so that the next generation is brought up in the Orchestra's tradition.

They have often tried to bring in the best principals from whatever other orchestras are in Vienna — but the player concerned has always remained a foreign body. One exception are the bass tubas, which, oddly, do not seem to 'grow' in Vienna. Above all it is the strings who are almost always sought out for the Orchestra by their teachers and introduced through rehearsals. In recent times some splendid young woodwind and brass players — also from Vienna — have joined the Orchestra.

I am often asked what is the difference between this Viennese orchestra and other first-class orchestras, and I usually answer thus: I believe that in inspired moments, sparked off by a conductor it likes and with whom it has a profound relationship (it is also possible for a good conductor to have no relationship at all with an orchestra), the Vienna Philharmonic far excels itself and demonstrates a level of musical performance unique in the world. Both in Vienna and on tour I have myself experienced the extent to which the Vienna Philharmonic is capable of this, particularly in the classical repertoire for which they have a special fondness. Even applying the highest standards, I can hardly imagine finer performances of Bruckner, Beethoven or Mozart.

This dual function of the Orchestra both in opera and concert has one disadvantage, however: 'familiarity breeds contempt'. With a change of musicians between almost every performance it can happen — particularly with a conductor to whom they do not feel specially inclined or whom they have inwardly rejected — that their standards sink below a certain level.

A purely concert orchestra has an easier time of it compared to a concert *and* theatre orchestra precisely because it only plays concerts throughout the year, which means that for every concert — particularly since the orchestra will have several guest conductors — it will have at least two or three rehearsals. The front-rank American orchestras, for example, have three or four rehearsals every time, so that a certain quality is guaranteed from the outset. Even the Berlin Philharmonic, if it plays Beethoven, which it knows to the nth degree, has three rehearsals, so that performances of these works can never become as sloppy as a repertoire opera. It is also the case, of course, that even with a good orchestral line-up a repertoire opera can suffer a drop in standards if there are bad singers on stage. And it is an unfortunate fact that there are not always first-class singers on stage, depending on the circumstances at the time. If in such a case, the orchestra is more or less condemned to play a meaningless accompaniment, it becomes unwilling and indifferent and so falls far below its own standards.

KARL BÖHM
A Career in Pictures

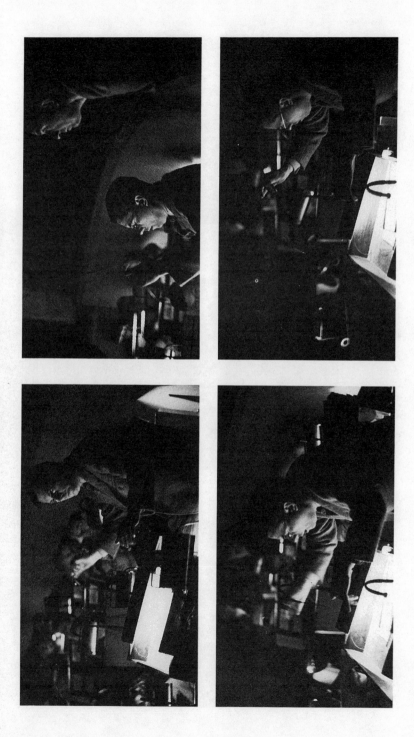

CHAPTER SIX

Richard Strauss — Extended Terzetto—
Magician at the piano —
Rehearsals before the Première —
Dresden, the Strauss Theatre — The sketch-books —
The creative process —
The scandal of *Die schweigsame Frau* —
Daphne— Eightieth birthday —
Strauss and Mozart — Atonal *Elektra* —
Richard Strauss's artistic testament—
Four last songs —
Death and Transfiguration — The funeral

On June 11, 1944, Richard Strauss celebrated his eightieth birthday in Vienna. Knowing this man of genius was of the utmost significance for me.

My relationship with the great composer — at the outset purely formal — began in my native city of Graz. I experienced one of his operas, *Der Rosenkavalier*, as a listener in the Graz State Theatre alongside my teacher Franz Weiss who used to play second harp. I was the *répétiteur* in *Ariadne*, having to rehearse all the roles and then take over the orchestral piano part. One can imagine how gripped I was by Richard Strauss, coming to this from the sounds of

Wagner. But now I have to admit honestly that, despite the great popularity of *Der Rosenkavalier*, *Ariadne* was one of my favourite operas, alongside *Elektra*, and it remains so to this day. I find that Strauss achieved something quite unique in this opera: to make chamber music with thirty-six players and still, at the end, to make the orchestra sound a hundred-strong — only this really great man was capable of that! And when I look back today on the so very productive and interesting rehearsals with the *buffo* ensemble, the Naiads and Dryads and the Echoes (I analyzed them all harmonically and thematically with Kapellmeister Oskar Posa), then I cannot tell you how much I profited from this detailed study of the work.

It is the same with Strauss as with Mozart, whom he loved so much: one cannot alter a single note, a single dynamic without severely affecting the whole. I know how attached Strauss was to *Ariadne*, and, for this reason, I conducted this opera on the evening of his eightieth birthday in the Vienna State Opera.

In those days in Graz I had no idea, of course, that I should have the opportunity to get to know Richard Strauss personally, and I had conducted several of his operas before I came into personal contact with him.

In Munich it was this same *Ariadne* that had earned me my first great success with the public and the press. As was fitting for third and fourth conductors, I had to take over opera performances without any rehearsal, even, on one occasion, a *Rosenkavalier* at 24 hours' notice. There was no alternative, because Knappertsbusch was unable to conduct due to illness, and Robert Heger was not present. Luckily the singers had rehearsed the very difficult third Act so well that nothing untoward happened, and I was happy for the first time to conduct and build up to a climax my beloved Terzetto at the close of the opera.

One evening, after dinner, Richard Strauss played over this Terzetto to his wife (who, incidentally, was not fully appreciated by many people), after which Pauline, on whose judgement Strauss placed great value said, 'very nice, but much too short. It must last longer.' On the basis of these objections Strauss gave the Terzetto its present form.

In Darmstadt I conducted *Salome*, and in Hamburg *Elektra* and *Arabella*. Here I came into contact for the first time, by letter, with the Master whom I then came to know personally in Dresden during the celebrations of his seventieth birthday. Richard Strauss is misunderstood by many people. When he looked at you with those steely-blue — one might almost say peasant's — cunning eyes, one could read in them all his greatness, which one recognized, above all, when listening to him play the piano, as I so often had the opportunity to do. I have myself accompanied — and heard others accompany — his *Ständchen* perhaps a hundred times, but the nightingales never sang as they did when he sat at the piano. On occasion he did not mind changing the ending. I remember that he once simply left out the postlude to *Heimliche Aufforderung* when the audience began to applaud after the tenor's last notes.

He was fascinating — and his son confirms this — when he played over a new opera on the piano and gave forth in his croaky voice. It must have been a phenomenon similar to Richard Wagner, who, as is well known, spoke the worst kind of Saxon, which is Leipzig Saxon. Just imagine how he sang through the *Ring* or *Die Meistersinger* in this Saxon accent (incidentally, in contrast to Richard Strauss, he was an utterly miserable pianist) — but still it is said to have been an experience not to be missed.

I possess a picture of Richard Strauss sitting in my room in the Dresden State Opera playing *Die schweigsame Frau* to me for the first time. There are certain passages that I have never again heard as they were in the Master's so utterly unadorned playing.

Strauss was very fond of me and my wife — and I may say the same of his wife. He once said: 'Why do I bother with you? You don't even play Skat!' We often walked for hours on end in the Erzgebirge in Saxony, where I had a weekend cottage. Sometimes it was quite impossible to follow Strauss in every topic of his conversation: one had to be as well up in literature as in music to be able to hold one's own with him. He was as at home in German literature as no other musician. I know from his son and his daughter-in-law that in the last weeks of his life he read only Goethe; he knew *Faust* by heart. He was equally familiar with Russian literature, and I remember his comment: 'I don't understand what people see in Russian Communism: the Russian hasn't changed, you can read it all in Dostoyevsky: "He can do immeasurable good and immeasurable evil — but whatever, he is incredibly sensitive to art." '

At the rehearsals before premieres, Richard Strauss was the most impossible man (not to use a stronger word) you can imagine. He would fidget over every chord, every dynamic so that in several rehearsals of *Die schweigsame Frau* I had to stand up for myself. 'But Böhm,' he said, 'you know the singers must be understood!' The libretto was by Stefan Zweig, and he loved it even more than some texts by Hoffmansthal. 'Everybody must understand these words!' I replied: 'Herr Doktor, look at the score! How is Cebotari to get her words out through that?' Then he muttered something, took the score quietly, went across to the Hotel Bellevue (which was sadly destroyed during the air raids) opposite the Dresden Opera, took a red pen, crossed out doublings, turned a *mezzo-forte* into a *piano* — and then the voices could be understood word for word.

The older he became the more his main interest in an operatic performance was to demand — as set out in his Preface to *Capriccio* — that the conductor must accompany the singer's words in such a way that they can always be understood. Now, that is uncommonly difficult in many works, if not impossible, as in *Elektra* for instance, of which he himself said: 'In *Elektra* I have gone to the furthest limits. From that point there is no going any further, only back.' And then, from an orchestra the size of that for *Lohengrin*, he went back to the chamber orchestra — *Ariadne*, *Capriccio*.

When writing down an opera Strauss naturally had a precise idea of how certain passages were to sound, and if, at rehearsal, one passage or another did not completely correspond to what he had imagined, he ceaselessly criticized it and made corrections, but nothing satisfied him. On such occasions he really did not show his best side, but I willingly accepted it from such a personality because I learned such an enormous amount from him. By contrast, with operas that had already been performed he was sometimes unbelievably generous towards me — not to say careless. On the other hand again, he was capable of taking as much pleasure in these operas as an *ingénu*. I shall never forget a performance of *Elektra* in Dresden. He was sitting in my box alone with my wife. In the Orestes scene he took her hand and kept hold of it, saying at the end: 'I had quite forgotten that I wrote it myself.'

It is well known that Dresden had for some time been the scene where premieres took place, where the works of Richard Strauss had their greatest successes. He found there a compatriot of mine, the famous Grazer, Ernst von Schuch, whom, sadly, I never heard, but who must have been a great orchestral trainer, for Strauss would not otherwise have written him such laudatory epistles. Ernst von Schuch put Richard Strauss on the agenda at a time when his name was not yet known. What he did for him broke new ground, and may be compared with what Kleiber achieved with the Berlin production of *Wozzeck*.

First *Feuersnot*, then *Salome* were performed. Older members of the Dresden State Opera told me, on the subject of *Salome*, that all the singers declared: 'This stuff is unsingable, you'd only wreck your voice with it. . .' Schuch made one more rescue bid and called a piano rehearsal in the Dresden State Opera. They were all there, with the exception of Herodes. On that occasion it was sung by Carl Burian, a Czech and, as I recall, one of the best Heldentenors there has ever been. Once more there were arguments with the singers: 'We can't sing that . . . we can't learn that. . .' Alongside Salome, Herodes has the hardest part to learn. Suddenly Burrian came in. Schuch, who addressed all the singers in the familiar 'du' form, except when he was cross, said: 'Hey, Burrian, late? You won't have the slightest idea of your part.' To which Burrian replied: 'I know my part by heart.' And he proceeded to sing it faultlessly, without a score. That put his other colleagues to shame. The ice was broken, and there was nothing to hinder further rehearsals for the première.

Ernst von Schuch's son told me a revealing story about the public dress rehearsal for *Salome*. In the Dresden Court Opera there were always public dress rehearsals in front of an invited audience at which the front six rows had to be kept free. There in the front row behind Schuch sat Richard Strauss — all alone. After Salome had been slain by the soldiers, and the curtain had come down, there was a deathly hush in the audience. The house-lights came up, but the silence held. Then Strauss stood up — and he was tall enough — turned around and said smilingly to the audience: 'I dunno — I liked it!' The spell was broken.

Elektra had its first performance under Schuch and after *Elektra*, in 1911, *Der Rosenkavalier*. This *Rosenkavalier* was a success the like of which one can scarcely imagine any more. There were special '*Rosenkavalier* trains' from Berlin which only carried people from Berlin to Dresden who could produce tickets for the performance; they travelled back to Berlin the same night.

The production had been given one hundred and ninety-nine times when I came to Dresden, and as I have mentioned, I conducted the two hundredth performance on Richard Strauss's seventieth birthday.

The cultivation of Strauss in Dresden was continued under Reiner and then Busch with *Intermezzo* and *Die Ägyptische Helena*; *Ariadne* and *Die Frau ohne Schatten* were first performed in Vienna. The first version of *Ariadne* was produced by Max Reinhardt at the Stuttgart Theatre (which was reopened with the same work) while the new version with the staged Prologue — which I love and find especially delightful, because, as Strauss once told me, in the figure of the Composer the touching form of Mozart hovered before Hoffmansthal — received its first performance under Schalk at the Vienna State Opera.

I have in my possession four of Richard Strauss's sketchbooks. He used to go for walks always carrying one of them, regardless of the weather. Often he would give his family, who frequently accompanied him on his walks, a particular sign: then they were to go on ahead or stay behind, and he would take the sketchbook and make notes. From these precious sketchbooks he would write the short score which was the final stage before the writing out of a full score, which would then require no further alterations.

My most precious souvenir is a sketchbook containing the sketches for part of *Ariadne auf Naxos*: it goes from the first half of the Prologue where the Music Teacher says, '*Ich weiss nicht wo mir der Kopf steht*', in exactly the right harmony, the vocal part with the right text and notes. Not one of them was later changed and the whole thing was more or less like a piano score. The book was so thick that I thought it must go beyond the Prologue, but I was mistaken, for, at the same time as Strauss was writing the final version of *Ariadne* he was also working on *Die Frau ohne Schatten*. The whole Empress scene in the third Act with the first draft of the violin solo is in this sketchbook in pencil form.

Strauss always used to say to me: 'I don't know why people always get upset about my Skat playing. Y'see, my dear fellow*, when I am playing Skat that's the only time in my life I'm not working.'

It is difficult to speak to an artist about the creative process. Firstly, this process is carried out under the surface and is thus removed from the actual ability of the creator to assess it; and secondly it evokes within him an inner reluctance to speak of it and to expose his secrets to the world. On just one occasion Strauss said to me in Garmisch: 'I have often thought to myself, you must do some more work after dinner, and I went on and on writing — nothing happened. Then I would go to bed, sleep soundly, go into my study after breakfast and find the solution, and everything was clear. So the creative process continued through the night.'

He would write out the full score from the short score with everything, even new counterpoints in ink in the final draft; very shaming — he never crossed anything out. If he made a mistake he would take a pen-knife, carefully erase it, smooth the spot with his nail and write the note over the spot. But there were very few corrections to be done, for he rarely made a mistake; particularly with transposing

---

* '*Schauen'S, Böhmerl!*' — Strauss's use of the diminutive form of Böhm's surname while retaining the formal 'Sie' rather than 'du' implies more intimacy than might the direct English equivalent of 'Smithy', for example; it does not however indicate the extreme familiarity of, say, 'Charlie', which both would have found improper. German forms of address still had such nice shadings of formal familiarity. (Tr)

instruments, where it is easy to go wrong. He would write just as the likes of us would write a letter.

Once he was sitting at his desk, with me behind him. He was working on the score of *Daphne* and discussing a Mozart interpretation with me. Upon which I said, 'But Herr Doktor, you can't talk to me about other things while you are working.' 'Don't worry, carry on, my dear Böhm,' he replied, 'I am able to think of the two things at once.' One should not forget that in his day, in addition to his composing activities in Berlin, alongside Leo Blech and Karl Muck, he was conducting over a hundred performances of repertoire opera a year while at the same time (as Muck related to me) conceiving *Ein Heldenleben* in his head.

There's one funny story I must relate here. The Intendant in Berlin was always pestering him that he should at long last perform a Meyerbeer opera, and Strauss simply would not. Finally he said: 'Fine, I shall prepare *Robert le Diable*,' thinking at the same time that without cuts it would last five hours and would soon be abandoned. Despite all expectations, however, it was a huge success, so that to his great annoyance he had to conduct this opera several times in the course of the season.

On the subject of the première of *Die schweigsame Frau* in Dresden: it was a frightfully hot summer, and we had to hold the rehearsals in killing heat in the rehearsal room under the roof. Strauss could not easily bear the heat, but he was tireless. Cebotari was capable of rehearsing for ten to fifteen hours, she was a model of discipline. She never played the prima donna and really got stuck into her part. She was discovered by Busch, but — apart from Mimì — only sang smaller roles with him as she had only been a short time in the theatre. Old Plaschke, well over sixty, sang the huge part of Morosus. The producer Josef Gielen, very young and highly gifted, came from Dresden Theatre. Strauss was very pleased about the progress of the rehearsals and wrote one happy letter after another to his wife Pauline, asking her to come as soon as possible. It should be known that Strauss put on *Die schweigsame Frau* against the will of the current Nazi regime, because a 'non-Aryan', Stefan Zweig, had, at the request of Richard Strauss himself, written the text after Ben Jonson.

Everything went splendidly up to the dress rehearsal. After this rehearsal Richard Strauss was playing Skat in the Hotel Bellevue with Tino Pattiera (the celebrated Dresden State Opera tenor; a strikingly handsome Dalmatian with a fine voice, there was no-one like him for being a ladies' man), Friedrich von Schuch and the long-serving costume designer, Leonhardt Fanto. While they played, Strauss didn't utter a word except for what related to the game. Suddenly he said to Schuch, 'I'd like to see the brush-proof of the poster for *Die schweigsame Frau.*' Schuch was quite astonished, he also had a bad conscience which was aroused by Strauss's unexpected interest, although he was not personally involved, and evaded the question. Then Strauss said, 'I'm not going to play any more until I've seen the proof,' and had it brought to him. As Strauss had rightly surmised, the name of Stefan Zweig was missing from the poster.

Strauss threw the proof on the floor and said: 'If Zweig's name is not printed, I'm leaving tomorrow.' He stopped playing Skat and, immediately, with all the naivety of a great genius, wrote a letter to Zweig who, by that time, had already emigrated. The letter is known well enough. Strauss pilloried the Nazi governor, particularly in this well-aimed sentence: 'For me there are two categories of people: those who have talent and those who have none, and for me the *Volk* exists only at the moment it becomes an audience. Whether it consists of Chinese, Upper Bavarians, New Zealanders or Berliners is a matter of indifference to me if they have paid the full price for their tickets. . .' He sealed the letter and took it down to the letter-box in the Bellevue himself and posted it. Naturally this letter was in the hands of the Gestapo by midnight at the latest.

The next day all hell broke loose. The entire government was supposed to be coming to the première. Now they were all advised to stay away. Only Goebbels could not be reached. They caught up with him only after he had boarded the plane to Dresden, so they informed him by radio, and the plane immediately turned back.

Strauss had to resign as President of the Reichsmusik-kammer [Reich Chamber of Music], and *Die schweigsame Frau* was cancelled after four performances. After the première the usual party was held in the hotel, which was attended by Herr Hanfstaengl as the only government representative, thought to be a dyed-in-the-wool Nazi (he came from a famous Munich family of art dealers). At this party he made a speech about the qualities of *Die schweigsame Frau* — including the text — and berated the government to such a degree that I said to my wife afterwards, 'in a week he'll be either in a concentration camp or in Switzerland.' A short time after that he was, indeed, in Switzerland.

The next Strauss opera to have its first performance was *Daphne*, in 1938. One day, shortly before Christmas, Strauss wrote to me on a photograph of the Bernini statue of Daphne: 'I am getting on well with *Daphne*. Would it give you some little pleasure if I were to dedicate it to you as a Christmas gift?' I replied: 'What a silly question.' Then came a card from Taormina: 'Have just finished the score of *Daphne*.'

Pauline Strauss particularly liked this opera. Before the première there was once again the official dress rehearsal with the six empty rows. Behind me sat Richard Strauss, apart from his wife. And as I laid down the baton — she loved the transformation scene above all — she took my head between her hands, gave me a little kiss and said: 'You're not getting a second kiss now, you're too sweaty.' On that occasion I performed *Daphne* together with *Der Friedenstag*. I would never do that again, because *Daphne* on its own is substantial enough, and *Der Friedenstag* remains a more or less occasional work and a pipe-dream.

After the public performance, together with Strauss, I visited his wife, who had had to stay away from the première because of illness. As Strauss slowly climbed up to the third floor he said of Pauline: 'Believe me, I really, really needed my wife. I actually have a lethargic temperament, and if it were not for Pauline, I shouldn't have done it all.'

That reminds me of a revealing scene in Garmisch, when Strauss said to Pauline: 'I'd like a Fachinger,' and she retorted, 'Get it yourself!' When I went to move the table back to stand up, she said, 'No, stay where you are, he can climb over the bench and get it for himself.' And then, when he was outside, she said to me: 'It does him good to move about, you know.' A small event but one that helps to explain a lot in vindication of her.

The last time I saw him was during his exile in the Palace Hotel in Montreux when he was already badly affected by his bladder trouble, and Pauline was looking after him so faithfully. One could not imagine a more beautiful thing at that age. I said to my wife, 'when one of them dies, the other will not survive for long.' And so it was.

On his eightieth birthday the Strauss's showed very much their old, intimate familiarity to my wife and me. 'Come on, Böhm. I'm fed up with all these celebrations. Why don't you come over to the Jacquinigasse?' So we went over to his home that same morning and witnessed all the congratulations. Then we drove to the Musikvereinssaal. My box was on the left-hand side, right where the conductor comes out. Strauss thought he had to go to the podium right away, but I said, 'Wait, just sit here, we've got a little surprise for you.' I conducted the *Meistersinger* Prelude and the *Rosenkavalier* Waltz, then Strauss came on to the podium, I gave a short birthday address and handed him a baton of gold and ivory adorned with a diamond. He took it — the baton was very heavy — and conducted *Till Eulenspiegel* with it. Afterwards, in the Artists' Room, he tapped me lightly on the shoulder with the baton and said: 'It's damned heavy, I shouldn't like to conduct *Götterdämmerung* with it. Give me another baton for the *Domestica.*'

At that point in the symphony which describes domestic relationships, where the theme of man and wife is heard, he looked at Pauline, and when the oboe d'amore enters for the first time and the birth of Franz is expressed in music he turned to 'Bubi', as he called his son all his life. Then follows the love scene between the couple and the merry battle, the wonderful double fugue. After that Vienna gave its Richard Strauss a tempestuous ovation.

It was June 11, 1944. That day there were no air raids, so the evening performance of *Ariadne*, with Strauss and his whole family in the audience, could take place in peace. For that evening I had sent tickets for a box to the former Social Democrat mayor of Vienna, Karl Seitz. I called him myself and asked him to be sure to come. He asked, 'don't you think that I, a political outlaw, would cause trouble for you?' And I replied, 'you were the mayor who conferred upon Strauss the Freedom of Vienna, so you are the man who ought to be there.' Upon which he did indeed come.

Richard Strauss remained a short while in Vienna, heard some of his operas and then finally returned to his villa in Garmisch until the end of the war.

After Bruno Walter awakened my love of Mozart, it was Richard Strauss who increased and deepened it. Strauss felt himself so closely bound to Mozart that he spoke of him in a manner I otherwise never heard this often apparently cold man use. He enthused over the unending wealth of melody of which Mozart was the inventor. As an example he cited Cherubino's second aria from *Figaro*. He told me of his great admiration for the genius of Mozart's unconscious technique of making transitions, and quoted an example from *Don Giovanni*: 'You remember, of course, the two *Adagio* bars in the finale of the first Act of *Don Giovanni*, after Leporello has invited in the masked figures, just before that tragic Trio? Look, my dear friend, if I had composed those two bars, I should gladly give three of my operas for them.' By that he meant that when a genius is so great that it needs only two bars of strings to make the transition from the liveliest *joie de vivre*, as represented in the Minuet, to the profoundest tragedy in the Trio, such mastery can never be excelled.

He once said to me, 'this Mozart came into the world complete, for he was capable of doing anything he tackled. He sat at the harpsichord and was able to play, he picked up a violin and was able to play it, he put a flute to his lips and was able to play it — not to mention his composing!'

I heard *Figaro*, *Così fan tutte* and *Don Giovanni* conducted by Strauss. On one occasion we travelled together from Garmisch to Munich, where he was conducting *Così fan tutte*. He said to me: 'I have often told you how one can always find the right tempo in a piece of music. I believe, at my age (he was then coming up to seventy-five) that I have finally found the right tempo. When a critic in Munich gave me bad marks for my tempi — one was too slow, one too fast — I wrote to him: "My respected friend, I have just read your review and I am delighted that there is someone who has received the correct metronome marks direct from Mozart in Musicians' Heaven. Would you be so kind as to tell me what they are?"'

Strauss usually did not do much in rehearsal and once,

when rehearsing a part of *Don Giovanni*, he gave an extra beat in a recitative where the Munich performers were used to going straight on. In the performance he forgot about it, was not ready and continued playing on the piano* in B flat while the tenor had already moved into another key. The leader made a sign to him, and he was back with them right away — he was unbeatable at improvising.

Once he was furious about a modern piece. 'Look, it is of no importance whether the clarinet plays another note here, or the oboe changes dynamic. Just try that in Mozart. In Mozart you can't make the slightest alteration in the dynamic, any idiot will spot it. Perhaps he won't know why, but he will feel uncomfortable. In Mozart a part of his genius is in the way he *forces* you; and that is how things ought to be!'

Strauss was an excellent practitioner of stagecraft. I don't need to underline that, because if you have read his correspondence with Hoffmansthal, you will know how much influence Strauss had in the shaping of the libretto as regards the building of a climax in the plot. As he told me one day, 'look at the stage, dear chap [*Böhmerl*], these days the 'over-dark' merchants are at work, not the 'over-lit' brigade! Let me tell you something that I experienced. The producer whom I admire the most is Max Reinhardt. One play he was producing opened with a scene in the middle of the night. And what did he do? To put the audience in the picture, the stage remained pitch black when the curtain went up, and then he played the scene fully-lit. Otherwise every change of expression on an actor's face, every gesture would be wasted if it was made in total darkness.'

Strauss placed great value on a text that was appropriate

* The keyboard continuo accompaniments to recitatives would have been performed on a piano, not on a harpsichord as today. It is still sometimes the practice in the opera house for the conductor to accompany the recitatives rather than the orchestral keyboard player. (Tr)

to the music. And I'd like to take this opportunity to deal with Mozart's textual repetitions which were once so criticized by dyed-in-the-wool Bayreuth adherents, and put forward just one of many opposing arguments. Here is an example that illuminates why Mozart repeats a passage again and again: it is the love duet between Konstanze and Belmonte from *Die Entführung*, in which, believing that they are to be executed at any minute, they declare their love for each other and then boldly look death in the face. The bars of this duet which crescendo to a *forte* with the same text repeated again and again have to be sung by the singers with the utmost intensity, and then its effect will not be lost: '*Mit der Geliebten sterben, ist seliges Entzücken. . .*' There is such a passage in *Die Zauberflöte* too, and, by the way, in Beethoven, in *Fidelio*, Act 2 Finale, where the build-up to a climax is achieved by the three different musical settings of Rocco's *Nur Euer Kommen*.

Strauss was a great devotee of Wagner, however. He often described himself as 'the last appendix of a great age.' Above all he loved *Lohengrin* with its brilliant A major, and *Tristan*. 'With *Tristan*, Wagner opened the door to the makers of new sounds, and I kicked this door wide open in the Clytemnestra scene in *Elektra* where I became partly atonal. And once, partly out of anger, because they were always screaming "renegade" at me, I said: "Look at the Clytemnestra scene, I've gone in for atonality myself!" '

During my exile in my room by the Attersee a messenger brought me the artistic testament of Richard Strauss, six pages written in his own hand. I find the suggestions which Richard Strauss gives in this legacy so precious that I wanted to make it publicly available, uncut, as I did once before in a book.*

---

* *Begegnung mit Richard Strauss* [Meeting with Richard Strauss], published

Richard Strauss suffered great mental torment under post-war conditions. I know this from many letters, but also from a personal visit to the Palace Hotel in Montreux, where I saw the Master for the last time. He feared that German theatrical culture would never recover from the almost total destruction of the opera houses and felt himself to be rejected and superfluous. Today, from Musicians' Heaven, he can smile, convinced that his pessimism was unjustified.

His son told me that he tried everything to stir his father, who had been used to working from morning to night throughout his life, out of the lethargy into which he had sunk. Thus it is to Dr Franz Strauss that we owe four of the loveliest songs with orchestra, that is to say the *Vier letzte Lieder*, that Richard Strauss ever composed. At that time in Montreux, Franz Strauss gave him three texts by Hermann Hesse and one by Eichendorff, and he started right away to set them to music.

When he later returned from his Swiss exile to the villa in Garmisch, I received a photograph of him which showed me clearly that the great master's will to live had finally been broken. As his son and daughter-in-law later told me, just twenty-four hours before his death, as he once again came out of unconsciousness, he said to 'Bubi', 'I can tell you now that everything I wrote in *Tod und Verklärung* is absolutely right: I have gone through just that experience in these past hours.'

In this tone poem, the extinction of a man is portrayed. Memories of youth rise to the surface, great plans are seized upon, but Death's door is always facing him. Finally the

and edited by Eugen Dostal, Verlag Doblinger, Vienna and Munich 1964. [Author's footnote] man dies and, transfigured, passes into the endless universe from which he has come.

Richard Strauss gave instructions in his will that the Funeral March from the *Eroica* and the Terzetto from *Der Rosenkavalier* were to be played at his funeral. Because of difficulties in getting permission to leave the country, I was unable to attend the funeral, which took place in Munich, but I know from eye-witnesses that Mrs Pauline Strauss, to whom we owe its final form, maintained her composure up to the end of the Terzetto, but then collapsed. Despite their very different characters I knew how deeply these two human beings were bound to each other and knew, too, that the one remaining could not long survive. A few months later Pauline Strauss died.

CHAPTER SEVEN

Wagner — Wieland Wagner — Dr Karl Muck —
Working in Bayreuth — The beginnings of recording —
The Dresden State Opera as a studio —
'Short playing' — The Bayreuth *Tristan* on records —
Recording techniques

Although I was always conducting Wagner, while in
Munich I felt inwardly somewhat distanced from him.
That may have something to do with the fact that the Nazis
made so much of him, and that one reacted defensively
against that — for it was well known that Hitler was a great
admirer of Wagner. I heard the most macabre travesty of
this musical predilection of Hitler's from an old usher at the
Berlin State Opera: in the middle of *Tristan*, which he
designated his favourite opera, Hitler had signed death
warrants in the back of his box after the first Act.

After the war I found my way back to Wagner and I even
intended to revive the *Ring* during my first period as
Director in Vienna. I had heard a great deal from Knappertsbusch about Wieland Wagner's talents as a painter
and I wrote to him: 'Would you like to make some designs
for a new production of the *Ring*?' Shortly after, a letter
came with designs for a complete *Ring*, already with its

famous 'disc'*, together with a splendid accompanying
letter in which he said that he would not only do the designs
but would also produce. Sadly both the letter and the
designs were lost in the fire at the Vienna State Opera.
Wieland later recalled this and repeatedly invited me to
work with him in Bayreuth. 'I very much want to do *Tristan*
with you in Bayreuth,' I replied. 'If you do a new production, I shall definitely keep myself free from commitments
in Salzburg, where I have had my home for almost thirty
years.'

For I had long been closely linked to Bayreuth, if
indirectly, through two people; my father and Karl Muck
in his time at Graz. Muck, who had formerly been conductor of the Boston Symphony Orchestra, returned to Graz
from internment in America during the First World War to
recuperate, and stayed there for a few weeks in a sanato-
rium. At that time I was rehearsing my first *Lohengrin*, but
only wanted to do it with a large chorus, while the one at
my disposal was so small and meagre. So I made it my
business (and this is the kind of thing you only do when you
are young) to prepare the Graz Male Choir — then in the
hands of my beloved teacher Franz Weiss — for the
performance, with seventy rehearsals. The rehearsals went
well, but the choir, unused to learning things by heart,
found that difficult, and in the beginning the acting got
nowhere. Wieland Wagner later had the choir remain
motionless — that would have made things much easier for
me then, but the producer had them running back and

* Wieland Wagner (1917–1966) was the grandson of Richard Wagner
and from 1951 until his death he co-directed the Bayreuth Festival with
his brother Wolfgang. His productions moved away from realism
towards symbolism. In the 1960s, for his production of the *Ring*, most of
the action took place on a disc or saucer-shaped platform which could be
tilted or split. The stage area was largely defined by means of lighting,
and the meaning of the drama was symbolically expressed by the use of
colour, geometrical shapes and designs. (Tr)

forth in the Swan Chorus. There were a hundred-and-forty men plus a hundred women in the choir — such a chorus had never been heard in Graz! Later, after the first wave of enthusiasm, it gradually broke up, and when I left Graz the members of the Male Choir were no longer taking any part in it.

Dr Muck attended the first performance and afterwards he sent for me and said: 'Now then, Herr Böhm, even if you did conduct *Treulich geführt* [the Wedding March] like a polka, you're still very gifted, and if you like, you may visit me in Maria Grün, and I'll give you a few authentic Bayreuth tips on Wagner.'

Twice that week I went to him with my scores, and Muck went through them with me, page by page. I thanked him profusely, for his hints were indeed invaluable. He played a major role in my life — through his wisdom and profound knowledge of Wagner, which he had obtained from Cosima. He told me how this brilliant woman, whom he knew well and with whom he had conversed on the highest level, had continued to astonish him right into her old age with her intelligence and liveliness. To show what this woman was made of, he told me the following story. On one occasion they were arguing about a passage by some philosopher or other and by midnight were still unable to agree. Then Muck drove back to his hotel. Later that night he was awakened by pebbles being thrown at his window. He got up and went to the window. Down below was Cosima Wagner sitting in her chaise, calling up to him: 'I've got the book here, come down, I *am* right!' He had to go downstairs in his pyjamas, where the elderly lady proved to him, using the book, that she was right.

Muck talked to me about the acoustic conditions in Bayreuth, and said to me, even then, 'you ought never to lose yourself in the "mystic abyss". You can never be too loud with the orchestra in relation to the stage. You can turn it right up, but you'll never cover even a singer with a weak voice: that is the miracle of Bayreuth.'

As a young man I had the opportunity of observing two extremely contrasted conductors, Bruno Walter and Karl Muck. When I think how differently they played the Sword motif — and I heard *Die Walküre* from both of them. Bruno Walter conducted the Sword motif with gentle gestures, the resultant sound was less dramatic than with Muck, who conducted it with dagger thrusts — but on the other hand the lyrical passages of *Die Meistersinger* or *Tristan* suited Bruno Walter better, and he radiated far greater warmth than Muck.

In 1961 Wieland Wagner made me an offer to do a new production of *Tristan* with him in the Bayreuth Festspielhaus. This time I insisted on a cast with Birgit Nilsson as Isolde and Wolfgang Windgassen as Tristan, who were singing the great heroic roles with Wieland Wagner anyway. Wieland once remarked jokingly: 'When Windgassen is no longer able to sing, we'll have to hang up a sign outside the Festspielhaus — "Closed today and for the next few years due to lack of a tenor".'

These rehearsals for *Tristan* were among the greatest artistic joys I have been granted in my life. Working with Wieland Wagner was harmonious in every respect. He took notice of what I wanted and did not, as some have suggested, produce in an 'anti-musical' way. On the contrary. For example, he placed the lovers' bank in the second Act not upstage but right at the front; and he did more than that. He made a phallus-like backdrop, inspired, I believe, by a tombstone for Tristan which he discovered in Cornwall, and this backdrop strengthened and amplified the reflection of the sound. The performance was — from the point of view of the staging as well as the musical performance — such a success that its fame spread far beyond the borders of Germany and Europe.

Our collaboration gave Wieland such pleasure, too, that he invited me to do *Die Meistersinger* with him the following year. In this *Meistersinger*, as opposed to his first production which I only know from pictures, he made a hundred-and-eighty degree turn. One had heard that in the first production, the Festival Meadow was an auditorium in which the chorus was seated, that is to say relatively motionless, while just one dancer (Kreutzberg) represented the element of motion. In the new performance of *Meistersinger* with me, he gave his temperament full play, turning that joke on its head, so there was a tumult on the Festival Meadow.

For the centenary celebrations of *Die Meistersinger* in 1968, Wieland Wagner wanted to do his third production with me. He had made the set models, as was his practice, and they were somewhere between the second and third stage in planning. Due to his all-too-early death, which I regretted as scarcely any other, this plan came to nought.

Previously there had come an invitation to produce a complete new *Ring* with him. I had not conducted the *Ring* since Dresden and, as well as chosing the cast, made it a condition that there should be a free day between *Walküre* and *Siegfried* since this was in the interests of the singers (especially Wotan and Brünnhilde). My suggestion was accepted, and this system, which proved to be *very* beneficial for everyone, has been retained.

So I conducted the *Ring* and took care, as did Wieland Wagner, to reduce the whole cycle to a human dimension, free from all over-Romantic ballast, in which I appear to have succeeded, for a famous Munich critic asked me in an interview how I had managed to find an entirely new style in *Rheingold*, a style that was no longer boring for a modern audience. I replied that I could only suppose that, having long been distanced from Wagner and the *Ring* and through my intensive preoccupation with Mozart and Bach, I had found something like a Wagner style refined through Mozart and Bach.

My favourite memories of recording are linked with Bayreuth, and I shall relate them in detail later.

My first gramophone recording was in the distant past. On the occasion of a concert with the Dresden Staatskapelle in Berlin, still in the wonderful Philharmonie in the Bernburger Strasse, I received an offer from the Electrola Company. I was to remain in Berlin the following morning to make at least one record. Since neither I nor the Staatskapelle had ever made a recording, I naturally declared my readiness to do so. Of course, in those days a record had a short playing time, that is, there was to be five minutes' music per side at the most. We recorded two pieces by Lortzing; the clog dance from *Zar und Zimmermann* and the ballet music from *Undine*. This was followed by a further invitation from Electrola to the Staatskapelle and me to make more records. I happily agreed but requested that the recordings be made in the Dresden State Opera, which had such splendid acoustics. They put in a special installation, namely a wooden acoustic panel for the brass who were the only ones to be seated on the stage, while the orchestra pit, which was equipped with hydraulics, was raised to the level of the stalls. We thus achieved some excellent recordings.

I remember an amusing story about the recording of the Reger Mozart Variations, which I am personally very fond of, and during which, as with all the records, we could only record for about four-and-a-half minutes per side. Now, I had frequently rehearsed each variation and was obliged to stop at a particular spot; the flute had to stop too, and I warned the gentlemen in advance by saying, 'I shall raise my arm at the moment when the recording stops.' The recording went particularly well, I raised my arm and the flute player, who was otherwise outstanding, played two more notes, upon which I said in my best Austrian accent, *'Das ist ja scheusslich'* ['That's terrible!' — an Austrian would pronounce it *scheiss*lich, however. — Tr] Two minutes later the recording' producer came out, laughed and said, 'Come and hear it for yourself.' I only heard the first four syllables: the *–lich* had been cut off. [So that he was heard to say 'That was shit!' (Tr)]

We then recorded the whole of the third Act of *Die Meistersinger* — I believe it came to fifteen or sixteen sides. That was unpleasant, if only because one had to keep on 'reheating' the atmosphere. Hermann Nissen from Munich — who retired only recently — was Sachs. This recording created a furore, especially in America. Margarete Teschemacher sang Eva; Torsten Ralf, Stolzing, and Elisabeth Höngen, Magdalena. Much later they stuck these old records together to make a long-playing record, on one side of which they could put about twenty-five minutes' music. This record was soon being brought out in America and is always regarded by the press as the best recording of the third Act, despite other complete recordings of *Die Meistersinger*.

Around that time, by the way, I also recorded the Pfitzner C major Symphony. After the war I once again met the Dresden Staatskapelle for recordings, which this time were made in a rather dilapidated church. The first thing I recorded with the 'Strauss Orchestra', as the Staatskapelle was called, was *Ein Heldenleben* and then the *Alpensymphonie*, the complete *Rosenkavalier* without cuts, and finally also *Elektra*.

After an interval of recording for His Master's Voice I conducted for Decca, because this firm had the Vienna Philharmonic under contract. About ten years ago I concluded a contract with the Deutsche Grammofon-Gesellschaft who made the Berlin Philharmonic available to me. There, from the classical repertoire, I conducted four or five Beethoven symphonies — sadly no Bruckner — then the complete series of the Mozart symphonies, which were currently in progress, including for the first time the little early symphonies and based on detailed studies of the latest research. (There is now a Mozart Edition published by the Internationale Stiftung Mozarteum in conjunction with Bärenreiter-Verlag.)

We recorded the following operas: *Die Zauberflöte, Don Giovanni, Così fan tutte* (His Master's Voice) *Tristan und Isolde* with the Bayreuth Festival Orchestra, *Daphne* (a live recording of the complete opera made during performances in the Theater an der Wien with the Vienna Symphony Orchestra) and finally *Die Frau ohne Schatten*, which I should really like to describe as historic. I prepared this opera especially for the Vienna Festival, and the General Secretary of the Vienna Philharmonic, Helmut Wobisch, urged that this freshly-rehearsed and well-rounded performance should be captured on records as soon as possible, because it would involve enormous costs to record it again in the studio. We recorded the opera in the Musikvereinssaal in ridiculously few sessions in a way which still brings me pleasure, since the achievements of the Vienna Philharmonic as well as the singers were so splendid. I have also recorded *Also sprach Zarathustra*, the *Festliches Präludium* and the *Vier letzte Lieder* by Strauss.

When they asked me to record *Tristan*, I made it a condition that it should be done 'live' in Bayreuth. 'Live' is not to be taken quite so literally in this case, for here it refers to a special recording technique. Given that almost all of the singers in *Tristan*, especially the singers of the two principal roles, must necessarily show signs of fatigue in the third Act (with one sole exception: Birgit Nilsson — I never saw this unique soprano tire vocally), we planned to record each Act on a different day (the idea was originally my son's, by the way). First, *Tristan* was thoroughly rehearsed with the Bayreuth Festival Orchestra and the singers; then, for the recording of each individual Act about a thousand people who it might be assumed would keep really quiet were seated in the Bayreuth Festspielhaus. Normally the Festspielhaus seats about two thousand people, but the technicians had discovered that it is irrelevant to the acoustics whether there are one or two thousand people in the theatre.

And so we recorded one Act of *Tristan* on each of three successive days with an audience of a thousand people each time, who were warned to keep especially quiet. Now you can just about imagine how each singer in the first Act, but above all in the great love duet in the second Act (without cuts, something, sadly, that I can rarely do outside Bayreuth), could really 'let rip' in the knowledge that there was no third Act to sing. I said to Windgassen at the time, 'in this recording you have set up a monument for later generations.'

We established something interesting in the process. In the second Act there was a breakdown, we had to stop, and you can tell in the course of the rehearsal/performance how difficult it was to crank it up again and re-establish the atmosphere.

We had two days' break, and then came the première. It was recorded 'live', as were the second and third performances. It was interesting that when we compared them with the recordings made during the public 'rehearsals' we had to make very few corrections. This was not because there were mistakes, but because the sound was better in places or the expression stronger: singers do not always feel the same. This *Tristan* recording was later honoured with several prizes.

Everyone who knows me as a musician is aware of how much value I place upon detailed study and the greatest possible perfection in rehearsal. But with a work such as *Tristan*, which has to be one long *crescendo* from the opening yearning A–F in the cellos to the final chord of the *Liebestod*, filled with the most gigantic passion, this can only ever be achieved in a 'live' recording. For this ultimate, decisive expression such a grand line is not possible with minute 'patch-work' in the studio. The Americans were the first to realise this, and they would often say, 'we'd rather have a record with a perfect line and one glitch than dull perfection smelling like something out of a can.'

In connection with this I should like to mention that my recording technique in the studio is aimed at recording the longest possible takes in one go (complete movements of symphonies, for example), and then to record the same piece at least once more in order to be able to make any necessary corrections to what was done before. I then listen to the piece in question with the record producer, tell him what does not sound right to me (certain instruments, especially the timpani and the bass drum are dangerous because of their wide dynamic range), we agree on technical and musical points and then it all proceeds until it is complete.

That is my way of working on orchestral recordings. In opera, however, there are many more components to be considered, and I have it put into my contract that no individual singer can decide at playback which of his takes should be used; only I can do that. For the whole recording may be splendid except for just one note of the tenor's not being quite as the singer intended it. If that note can be changed without risk, then, of course, that is done. If not, in respect to the quality of the whole, I have to overlook that note, for I am the only one in the position '*sine ira et studio*' to make a disinterested decision from a higher viewpoint.

CHAPTER EIGHT

1945 — The Vienna State Opera fire —
Flight to the West — Forbidden to work —
Exile in Graz — Pasetti — Jimmy Hands —
The 'Victorious Blood' — A pencil as a party badge

On a day which may be quite interesting for numerologists, that is, on 12.3.45, bombs fell on the old inner city of Vienna and, as well as other buildings and houses, hit the Vienna State Opera.

I was at home at the time with concussion sustained from a heavy fall. I had not obtained the 'emergency petrol' I had requested for my old DKW car, had been forced to go to the opera on foot and had slipped on some ice. My wife, who was out shopping, phoned to tell me that the air raid alarm had gone off. I told her to seek shelter in the cellar of the Vienna State Opera, since I regarded it as one of the safest in the old city, on account of its depth. A real inferno did indeed rain down on the old city that day, in splendid weather incidentally. The excuse that they had not wanted to hit the Opera but rather the North-West railway station really does not hold up.

My wife wanted to take some documents out of my office and was caught there in the raid. She was, together with a fireman who was later slightly injured, the first witness of the direct hit on the Opera. The iron safety curtain had in fact been lowered as a precaution, but the first bomb — containing high explosives — fell right on to the stage and the incredible blast from it pushed the safety curtain out into the auditorium. The next bombs to hit the auditorium, were a mix of high explosive and incendiary bombs; in a flash the whole of the auditorium was ablaze with phosphorous.

My wife was pulled into the cellar, her coat on fire. I learned of all this much later, of course, because shortly after she called, the phone went out of action. When I heard from people who had come from the inner city that the Opera was on fire, I went on, despite my condition, through the chaotic traffic and the burning ruins to the Opera. There I stood in front of the building until it was completely dark, for five or six hours I believe — the raid had happened at midday — weeping like so many fellow citizens of Vienna, people who perhaps had never been to the Opera in their lives and yet to whom it meant so much as a symbol.

Absurdly, I tried to drag valuable pieces of furniture out of the still burning building. We placed them opposite the Opera: the next day, of course, they were stolen.

Apart from anything else, the destruction of the Vienna State Opera meant for me that the idea of putting on concert performances of opera there was hopeless. I do believe, however, in spite of this — and the day of the collapse was drawing ever nearer — that none of the staff joined the armaments industry and certainly not the civilian militia.

The Russians were getting nearer and nearer, and I certainly did not want to stay in the city with my wife — my son was still in Switzerland. Firstly, because I am no hero by nature and secondly, because I no longer had any kind of artistic duties here.

So I fled with my wife to Traun near Linz, where I had a

dear friend who put us up for two weeks and then later, as I have said, to Käthe Dorsch on the Attersee.

This was the beginning of a terrible time for me. I had no scores with me whatsoever, not even a piano at my disposal. . . Then, one day — I believe it was the end of May — the Americans came. I can remember exactly how one could see with a telescope the tops of the tanks from the surrounding mountains. They came, but left us relatively unscathed. And on another day the messenger arrived to hand me Richard Strauss's testament. That was the first and the only piece of news I had from him. It was impossible to phone, and to travel there was out of the question. Within our zone we were, so to speak, voluntary prisoners. I could not even get in touch with my family who were living in Graz and in Velden on the Wörthersee.

Then Salzburg was given the order by the Americans to hold the 1945 Festival. I was engaged to conduct *Die Entführung* and two concerts. The Philharmonic could not get out of Vienna, of course, since the city was entirely under Russian administration. So, on that occasion, an orchestra made up of musicians from the Mozarteum Orchestra played. An acquaintance took me by car with him to Salzburg, where Baron Puuthon informed me: 'We are such old friends — it's so awful — I know your position — but the Russians insist. . .' The Russians had explained to the Americans that it was unacceptable for me to conduct at the Festival. In the meantime the Allies had also issued a ban against Krauss, Furtwängler, Knappertsbusch, who was in fact himself a victim of the Nazis, and Karajan.

This was the beginning of a really terrible time for me — and, probably, for all my colleagues. That good man Hans Moser, whom I chanced to meet in the canteen in Salzburg, exploded in rage over it all: even he had been banned for a period! What he, who was actually married to a Jewess, was supposed to have done, I have no idea. It was certainly one of the many misunderstandings around that time. He sat opposite me and said, 'if only they would let us perform! I'd forego the fee, but I must perform, I must be on stage!' I had never known this modest artist be so impassioned.

He was saying something that also applied to me and my colleagues: that earning money was not the most important thing, but the desire to share this gift that comes from somewhere, the talents that most of us have done our utmost to cultivate; to give people some pleasure.

I was like a caged animal pacing back and forth because it misses its liberty. When today I see a tiger or a lion pacing back and forth, I can look back and really identify with that poor animal. For with talent we are also given a duty to give a share of ourselves to mankind, and when this positive reaction is missing, and this need to give is blocked, then we are affected to the very depths of our nervous system.

I was then fifty-one years old, used to exercizing the profession of conductor from the age of eighteen and to sharing myself with others. I had striven all my life to give of my best and I stress that here again: I have always tried to give of my best, regardless of what the audience looked like. Naturally, sometimes I am on better or worse form, but there is always the intention to try and get the best out of myself.

So, from one moment to the next, I was out in the cold. When, later, I got to Graz, I was not even allowed to give lessons! And there were financial worries, too. Due to an unlucky investment in a lard factory in Dresden, in which I had placed all my savings — the interest they were supposed to send never arrived because of the war — we stood there, would you believe it, with just fifty marks to our name. And so we had to live on the lessons that my wife was giving. Karlheinz had in the meantime returned from

Switzerland. My brothers in Graz supported me, of course, but it was still hard to lose one's independence at such an age.

So there I was, called to Salzburg but then driving back to the Attersee, feeling depressed and thinking that the best thing would be if we were able to move back to my home town, since the British had occupied Graz (in fact the whole of Styria up as far as Semmering). When that became possible, we effectively had to start all over again. As I have said, I was not allowed to teach, I wasn't allowed to do anything whatsoever. The British were very nice and even put a concert my way — Bruckner's Fifth. How happy I was to have an orchestra in front of me again — the one in Graz (how long ago had I left them?). . . Then came another ban, because the British thought that, following the Allies' joint agreement, they ought not to grant me permission to perform, solely and simply because I had, after all, been Director of the Vienna State Opera.

As I stood there with my fifty marks, my trials really began. There were the so-called Denazification Commissions, and an American officer, Otto Pasetti, in Salzburg was given the task of handling my case, with many others. There is one good deed I must credit him with: he saw to it that my son was able to return to us from Switzerland. Karlheinz travelled back in a special repatriation train, and since I did not know its time of arrival, I was not even able to meet him — after a year and a half in which we had not seen each other. I was not even able to welcome him that evening, since he was so exhausted after his twenty-hour train journey that I didn't want to interrupt his deep sleep. But I shall never forget Pasetti for fetching my son at that time.

Pasetti was — and there is no other word for it — a frustrated tenor who had actually sung Parsifal before the war in Graz. There were several rumours flying about as to why he had emigrated to America (he was born in South Tyrol). Whatever it might have been, the one thing I hold against him is that he did not simply say to me, 'you're getting an eighteen-month ban from conducting' instead of raising my hopes from one week to the next, and the eternal coming and going almost drove me out of my mind. Possibly it was not his fault, but that of his superiors.

One day Bruno Walter, with whom I had kept up a regular correspondence, came to Vienna, got out of the aircraft, was welcomed, and his first question was, 'how is my friend Böhm?' whereupon everybody fell on a certain part of their anatomy — figuratively speaking, of course. When he heard that I was banned from performing, he asked, 'why?' 'We don't know.' 'What is he living on, then?' Walter persisted, 'has he got that much money saved?' 'As far as we know, his wife gives singing lessons.' Then he demanded that my wife should be engaged to sing the soprano part in the performance of Haydn's 'Seasons' that he was conducting.

Towards the end of my professional exile I became very, very friendly with the Music Officer, an Englishman called Jimmy Hands who later, when he was on a visit to Graz or Vienna, would stay with me. He was a heartwarming, dear person, who not only spoke brilliant German but also knew all the texts of Hugo Wolf's songs by heart — a considerable achievement! We were very much on the same wavelength, because he was himself so very musical. Although it counted as 'top secret', I asked him one day: 'Tell me, Jimmy, what have they got against me that means I cannot work?' And then I finally learned the reason. It had to do with a book by a certain Weinschenk; *When artists chat* . . .

And then I remembered. One day a certain Herr Weinschenk came to me and said: 'There are so many elderly artists, and I should like to write a book for them which contains anecdotes told by distinguished men.' So I told

him about the fourth or fifth performance of *Lohengrin* in
Graz, just at the exact moment '*Wer hier im Gotteskampf zu
streiten kam für Elsa von Brabant, der trete vor*', a black cat
stepped out of the Intendant's box, curled its tail, sat on the
prompt box, and then sauntered off. It was the biggest
laugh I ever got. I told him this story because it's not the
sort of thing that happens every day. Herr Weinschenk
went on to ask me, 'Weren't you in Munich at the time of
the march to the Feldherrnhalle?' 'Yes, yes, I had just
rehearsed two pieces that were later put on the "cultural
Bolshevism" list.' And in this connection I am supposed to
have said, 'during this rehearsal there flowed the blood that
was later to become so victorious.' This sentence is so
idiotic that I quite definitely never said it, but because it
was there in that book they used it against me.

The British wanted to allow me to conduct, but because
of the Allied Agreement they were not able to make such a
major decision.

My wife had spoken four or five times to the Russian Music
Officer at the Hotel Imperial who told her that he had in his
possession a picture of me in which I was wearing a gold Party
badge. (At the first performance of *Die Schweigsame Frau* I had
been given a gold pencil by Richard Strauss which I was
wearing proudly in my breast pocket.) When my wife replied,
'My husband was never in the Party. Take a close look, it is a
pencil. Get a magnifying glass!', he had to admit that he was
mistaken. That's how it was.

After two years, permission finally came for all of us —
Furtwängler, Krauss, Knappertsbusch, Karajan and me —
and we were allowed to conduct again. Egon Hilbert was
then head of the Bundestheaterverwaltung*, and had done
an enormous amount for the rebuilding of the Staatsoper.

* Federal Theatres Administration, the body which controls the theatres
in Vienna run by the Austrian Federal Government, including the
Staatsoper, Volksoper, Burgtheater.(Tr)

One will never know how many forged passes he gave people to enable them to cross the Russian checkpoint at Enns.*

And it was Hilbert who right away invited me to conduct. I chose *Fidelio*.

* Post-war Austria was divided into zones governed by the Allied Powers: movement between zones was only possible with varying degrees of difficulty. (Tr)

CHAPTER NINE

Fidelio — Naples —
A small monument to Signor Imbruglia —
Mozart in Italy — Salome the cat —
Buenos Aires — A tenor sings the alto part —
The National Anthem in waltz-time — Berlin —
Wieland Wagner's *Aïda* — My eye operation

Fidelio, this finest of all operas, ends by opening out into an oratorio of humanity. After the outcome of the plot has long since been decided, Florestan is returned to his beloved Leonore, and Pizarro is led off for punishment. Only Beethoven was capable of such an achievement; of creating an ensemble and climaxing in a jubilant C major. What might have been a lessening of effect expresses in Beethoven an elevation into the Beyond.

Fidelio was the first opera score I received from my parents. As a five-year-old at my mother's side in the old Franzenstheater in Graz, it was the first opera I heard. And in 1920 I had my first great success with *Fidelio*. And now the first opera I was allowed to conduct after my two-year ban was *Fidelio*, in the Theater an der Wien, the temporary quarters of the Vienna State Opera. I chose this opera intentionally because — however blasphemous this may sound today — I identified deeply with Florestan and his imprisonment.

This return to my beloved art of self-giving was not that easy, however. At seven o'clock in the evening we were still not sure if I was to conduct or not, because there were still serious difficulties, due to politics, obstructing me. But the Theater an der Wien was in the French zone and at the pleading of my friend Mautner Markhof — I thank him for it to this day — the French general took steps to protect me, since there were open threats against me from certain quarters. So I was able to conduct this performance, if with my heart in my mouth, and to bring to it a successful conclusion — though I have to say that it was certainly not the best *Fidelio* of my life.

I have forgotten to mention that one day just after the war, when I was once again in a deep depression, I said to my wife, 'if I am ever again in the position of being allowed to conduct, I shall do all I can to build an international career so as not to be dependent upon my homeland which has laid a two-year conducting ban on me.'

So now I was conducting various performances at the Theater an der Wien, among them a new production of *Turandot* with Maria Cebotari in the title role and Helge Roswaenge as Calaf. As much as one could travel in those days, I had concert invitations from all over, among them an invitation from the Teatro San Carlo in Naples to conduct a new production of *Tannhäuser*.

I made a number of friends in Naples, many of whom remain friends today, despite the fact that it is a long time since I have been back. My best friend Signor Imbruglia unfortunately met his death in a terrible road accident. I single him out because he, as an Italian — on the premise that this is a great rarity — had a remarkably deep affinity with Mozart. He was a lawyer but had often written introductory articles on music and, among other things, founded that really splendid chamber orchestra in Naples which was later taken over by the radio. I conducted a few concerts with this orchestra too. This dear Italian friend came to me through Mozart. He was a regular visitor to the Salzburg Festival and, standing outside the stage door like many others, said in a German which compared with my inadequate Italian is of literary standard: 'I am a great admirer of yours, please come to Naples some time.' I later questioned this man in connection with Mozart — he knew all the piano and violin concertos which are listed in the Köchel catalogue and was singing and whistling all of the themes, including even those of all the symphonies. I mention this in such detail because I want thereby to erect a monument to this unforgettable, selfless friend.

In general the Italians have absolutely no affinity with Mozart, although he wrote almost all his operas in Italian. I have often asked myself the reason for this and have come to the following conclusion: they confuse him with Rossini — *Il Barbiere di Siviglia* has, indeed, the same characters as *Le Nozze di Figaro*, and this similarity of names leads the Italians to put Mozart on the same level as Rossini. Nothing against Rossini! Leaving aside his fantastic culinary art from which many cooks still profit to this day, I have to say: it is undoubtedly a stroke of genius that produces a work like *Il Barbiere di Siviglia* in so short a time, but the genius of Rossini is on quite a different plane from the genius of Mozart. I believe that this effectively bars access to Mozart for the average Italian listener. Generally, in my experience, among the Latins only one race understands and really loves Mozart, and that is the French.

So I arrived in Naples and was given an overwhelmingly warm-hearted reception. For five years I had the opportunity to get to know the Neapolitans. They are the dearest and best people I have ever encountered. That is in no way affected by the fact that when my wife and I went out into the suburbs where the poorest of the poor live, a three-year old lad made off with her purse while she was giving him a few pennies. One can be lied to a hundred times a day there, but that has no effect whatever on the feeling between us and the Neapolitans. On the other hand, they won't mind if one alludes to their wiles and dodges.

The weather was always magnificent, our whole stay was magnificent! However, one incident nearly spoiled my first appearance there. I had rehearsed *Tannhäuser*, and the sets were terrible. They had not been made, as in other cities, in their own studio or even in the same workshop, but simply ordered from Rome or Milan. You can imagine what they looked like. Everything was wobbly, even the trees, since it was all made of papier maché. I thought, 'what can I do? The music is the main thing.' But even so it was so sadly lacking that I finally declared to the theatre director that if the following day's rehearsal was no better, the performance could not take place. He calmed me with a torrent of words: 'It's always like this here, it always comes right at the last moment. ' The dress rehearsal was terrible, and I therefore forbade a *transmissione*, a broadcast, since I wanted the inadequate achievement to be confined at least to the Teatro San Carlo. The theatre director promised me, 'no *transmissione*.'

I get to the rostrum and the place is full of microphones for a *transmissione*. What was I — making my debut in the Teatro San Carlo, a famous theatre after all — to do? There was nothing for it but to start the *Tannhäuser* Overture.

It was the custom there that all the winds were seated on one side — the woodwind, the horns, trumpets and trombones — and on the other side all the strings and the harps. I was welcomed with an enormous ovation for a newcomer, began the Overture and somewhere around the twelfth bar I heard laughing from the gallery. 'Well, I've flopped already,' I thought. However nice they may be, they are as merciless as small children. If a tenor sings an unsupported falsetto note, they imitate him throughout the performance. I thought, 'I don't care,' turned encouragingly towards the cellos for their first entry, but never found out the reason for the laughter. When the Overture was over the audience applauded as if possessed, shouted 'encore' so loud that I thought the theatre would fall in. Lorenz was Tannhäuser, the famous Tebaldi was singing her first Elisabeth, in Italian in fact.

The Act was over. My wife came into my dressing-room and I said to her: 'I thought I'd flopped at the twelfth bar.' Then she told me, 'You couldn't see. It was a cat again, like in Graz.' A cat of almost historic significance. Welitsch had been singing Salome the night this cat was born, so it was given the name Salome and wore a red ribbon round its neck with a little bell. This Salome could put up with anything — except music. She was faithful to the Teatro San Carlo and caught numerous mice, but whenever she heard music she did a disappearing act. It was she who brought me success through laughter, for she jumped from a box into the orchestra pit and then went off in a huff.

The performance was excellent in terms of the local conditions — one could not expect it to compare with the standards at the State Opera. It was pretty much a sensational success and brought me a *Meistersinger*, a *Tristan* and a *Parsifal* in Italy. Later in San Carlo I did *Die Walküre* and the *Wozzeck* I have already mentioned. Of Mozart's operas I performed *Figaro*, *Don Giovanni* and *Così fan tutte*.

There followed an invitation to take over the German *stagione** at the Teatro Colón in Buenos Aires.

---

* The Italian word *stagione* literally means 'season'. In the context of opera houses, it refers more specifically to a season in which the operas to be staged are given a limited number of performances with a (largely) unchanged cast. This contrasts with the 'repertoire' system, in which productions continue for longer, but with a succession of changes of cast

I began my activities there in 1950 with a new production of *Die Walküre* and stayed for four years, that is up to 1953 as director of the German *stagione*. The work in Buenos Aires was not exactly light, since the orchestra then was not very homogeneous. Also the musicians were terribly badly paid and they had to give private lessons in the mornings. This did not exactly have a beneficial effect on afternoon rehearsals, which took place at the unhappy hour of 2 pm.

My favourite memory is the premiere of the opera *Jenůfa* by Janáček in 1950. I had prepared this work in the minutest detail, particularly with regard to dynamics, the markings for which are very incomplete. The cast was splendid, and the opera was such a success that it had to be repeated the following year. In 1951 I conducted the first performance [in Buenos Aires] of *Elektra*, with Christel Goltz in the title role. Besides the opera performances I conducted some concerts and in the same season gave the first performance in South America of Gustav Mahler's *Das Lied von der Erde*.

Shortly before the repeat of this concert the singer of the contralto part fell ill and was unable to appear. Since the concert was completely sold out, they asked me to do what I could to enable it to go ahead. So I turned to Lorenz Fehenberger, an incredibly musical man, who was the tenor at the Munich Opera and sang the tenor part in *Das Lied von der Erde*, and asked if whether, with the help of some changes, he might be in a position to take on the alto part. And so he did, and with great success — it was an achievement in any case, one which I might call rather unique. It is the only time in the history of music that a tenor has substituted for an alto, and I do not believe that many singers would be able to take over such a part in addition to their own.

and conductor. Each system has its advocates and its detractors. (Tr)

There is one tragic event that I have to recall at this point. On July 1, 1952, at the end of a performance of *Capriccio* in the Theater an der Wien I received the news of the death of my mother. We had always had a particularly close relationship, and I must confess that, in a state of nervous exhaustion after the performance, I almost collapsed. Whether that has anything to do with my later illness I do not know, but I am glad that my mother did not have to know about the serious eye surgery that I had to undergo on June 30, 1952 for a detached retina. Since the condition was only discovered late, the operation on my left eye was not one hundred per cent successful, the more so because eight days after the operation there was a haemmorage.

Despite this, in the middle of August, I flew with my wife to Buenos Aires (and in those days the flight lasted sixteen to eighteen hours) to conduct a new production of *Salome*. Then, true to the promise I had made to my friend Alban Berg, I rehearsed *Wozzeck*.

Nobody apart from myself was so utterly convinced that this work could enjoy success in a theatre which really favoured Italian opera. Most unusually, the German *stagione* gradually overtook the Italian, so that the demand for tickets for the German *stagione* finally became greater than for the Italian operas. Such a thing had never happened in the history of the Teatro Colón.

This theatre has in my opinion the best acoustics in the world, both for opera and for concerts, in which the orchestra is seated on the stage. As far as I know, it was built around the turn of the century when they had no instruments for measuring acoustics, but still the architect succeeded in creating, I should like to say, an acoustical miracle. One can hear equally well from every seat in the Teatro Colón.

To return to *Wozzeck*. The rehearsals were not easy.

Again, I had to have around twenty or thirty orchestra rehearsals — but the performance was recompense for all my trouble. Even during the rehearsal period there was so much interest, especially from one newspaper, that its arts editor took it upon himself, at his publisher's expense, to translate Büchner's text into Spanish. This idealist even had the translation distributed free at the premiere to a large part of the audience, as a result of which Büchner, whom the South American public were encountering for the first time, created as much interest as Alban Berg.

Because of its great success, this *Wozzeck* then had to be put on again the following season. In addition to *Wozzeck* I conducted in concert the Mozart *Requiem* and Beethoven's *Missa Solemnis*, which only Fritz Busch had conducted twice in Buenos Aires, with the excellent chorus of the Teatro Colón which was run by a really splendid chorus master, Boni, an Italian.

In 1954, I sadly had to give up my position at the Teatro Colón on account of my Vienna engagements, but ten years later, by way of a reward for my efforts, so to speak, I had the wonderful experience of making a guest appearance there with the Vienna Philharmonic. With an attractive programme and such a top-class orchestra it's no great work of art to make a success; but the reward came at the *beginning* of the programme when I stepped on to the rostrum. I was greeted by applause the like of which I had never experienced in all of my four years of *stagione*. Once again the principle and the experience which I have always had as an artist held true: everything comes round again! This applause, in advance of the performance, was doubtless their thanks for the pioneering work which I had carried out in this theatre.

At the last concert (there were four in all), when we had given two encores, and the audience still would not give up applauding, I thought quickly as I left the stage, 'How do I make the audience leave?' I then returned to the rostrum and said in Spanish: 'Now, by ways of thanks, we shall play you the Austrian National Anthem', upon which the audience rose to their feet as one and, deadly serious, awaited the new Austrian anthem, which practically nobody abroad knew. Instead of that, however, I had already agreed with the orchestra what we would play. I turned my back to the orchestra so that I could see the expression on the faces of the audience and gave the cue for the 'Blue Danube' waltz. As the horns' first notes sounded, and the audience recognized it, their expressions relaxed, they sank back on to their seats and cheered the end of this immortal waltz.

In Vienna I conducted fifteen to twenty opera performances per year, including a new production of *Capriccio* by Richard Strauss. Apart from that I busied myself with a stage version of Handel's *Judas Maccabeus* which was taken up by the Munich publishers, Verlag Edition Modern and now awaits its first performance. I made music regularly with the Vienna Philharmonic, for this connection remained unbroken from 1933 onwards.

After a few concerts in Berlin and other German cities, the 'proper' renewal of my acquaintance with Germany (not counting my performance of *Elektra* with which I opened the Deutsche Oper am Rhein in Düsseldorf) was in the context of the opening of the re-built Deutsche Oper in Berlin. In the course of the following years this association intensified to such an extent that, on my seventieth birthday, I was made an Honorary Member of the Deutsche Oper, and my bust, commissioned by the Senate, was made in Berlin and set up in the foyer.

In the course of the opening celebrations I conducted a new production of *Aïda*. This was remarkable above all because of the production by Wieland Wagner who shook the cobwebs from this opera just as he had from his grandfather's. You may agree or disagree with such experiments — for Wieland Wagner it was no experiment but his firm artistic conviction — but whichever it was, there is one thing to be said for them: they really shake up a more or less indifferent audience, and are worth it if only for the debates which come out of them.

For myself, I admit today that I was not utterly convinced by everything I saw on stage: but what a powerful effect this production had as opposed to another, more recent production of *Aïda* which I have seen; one so bound up in tradition that one had to declare unequivocally, 'this will not do!' That was the feeling of almost all of my friends who were informed about art. This production of *Aïda* with Wieland Wagner characterized our artistic collaboration which later had such endlessly fruitful results in Bayreuth with *Tristan, Die Meistersinger* and the complete *Ring*.

On a tour with the company of the Deutsche Oper Berlin in Japan I opened the Nissei Theatre in Tokyo. The programme included *Fidelio*.

In those post-war years — I should like to call this time from 1947 to 1955 my 'Years of Wandering' ['*Wanderjahre*' — an allusion to Goethe's novel *Wilhelm Meisters Wanderjahre* Tr]. With the exception of North America, I travelled almost the entire world. I have already related my work as artistic director of the German *stagione* in Buenos Aires which brought me such happiness.

It was also on the North American continent that a second dangerous eye disease flared up. On December 16, 1960 I was to give a Richard Strauss concert with the New York Philharmonic. The final rehearsal was to be that very morning. I conducted the orchestral works *Don Juan* and *Domestica* without a score, but had the impression that my vision was severely impaired. Then came the last piece, the closing scene of *Capriccio*, sung by Lisa della Casa as the Countess. As I opened the score I noticed that I could no longer see any sharp outlines clearly. I mentioned it to

Madame della Casa afterwards, who immediately rustled up a friend who knew an opthalmologist who lived near Carnegie Hall and drove me to him. This doctor established that there was a tiny tear in the retina, asked me who had operated on my other eye, put through an immediate call to Professor Böck in Vienna who advised me to come to Vienna for an operation right away. So I had to withdraw from the concert, which, willy-nilly, was taken over by two assistant conductors.

Here I must say something in unstinting praise of the Americans. I do not believe that anyone in Europe would have accepted my cancellation so unconditionally and in such a touching manner as did the management of the New York Philharmonic. I actually wanted to go on and conduct that concert, but after the doctor told me that I would then so extensively destroy the retina that I would never be able to read a score again, I flew back to Vienna the same evening. Dr Böck's car was waiting there to take me to the clinic.

Happily it turned out that the retinal tear was very small, and Professor Böck assured me that the operation would be successful. I had the operation on December 18 and afterwards was given the famous dark glasses. I remember precisely the moment, ten days later, when Professor Böck announced that he was going to remove the glasses. Trembling, I held my alarm clock, on which the date appears very small. I was even able to see these tiny figures again in sharp outline.

Professor Böck then examined me and he informed me that I had regained full vision in my right eye. At this point I should like to thank this wonderful doctor and human being who enabled me to continue to practise the profession I love so dearly.

CHAPTER TEN

Second summons to Vienna —
The opening Festival —
Concert of whistling before *Fidelio* —
Contract dissolved —
Deus ex machina: Rudolf Bing

My work as a guest conductor gave me a lot of pleasure, most especially because in the concert hall (as well as in the theatre, of course) I had enough rehearsal time to produce good performances. I had not the slightest expectation that I would be taking on a permanent appointment, except possibly the music directorship of an orchestra.

But now the question arose of the appointment to the post of Director of the Vienna State Opera — former Director Franz Salmhofer had declared that he would not take over as Director of the new Vienna Opera.

I have already mentioned that, when the Opera was burnt down, people who had possibly never been inside stood and wept in front of the burning building. The Opera has the love of the entire Viennese population, but this love conceals within itself dangers which have since become obvious to everyone. So, every time there is a change of Director, the talk is of reforms, but — how does it go in

*Palestrina?** *'Sie wollen, sie wollen die Reformen nicht!'* ['They don't want reforms, they don't want them!'] If you really start to make reforms but, for example, do not retain a less able singer or give him a less advantageous contract, you have straight away made enemies of his whole family and all his friends, and such enemies soon add up to a respectable number.

I had for some time been involved in negotiations with third parties over assuming the Directorship. I always took a negative position when such contacts were attempted, as I was particularly content with my travelling life and was very well aware of the intrigues and other unnecessary burdens associated with the appointment, however much it was gilded with the opening of the new Opera House. For these reasons I had even promised my wife that I would not accept the directorship of the Vienna Opera.

One day when I arrived back from a journey, I was met at the station by a friend who told me that the Council of Ministers was meeting right then to reach a decision on the appointment to the position of Director. I was to come to this ministerial meeting without fail. So that's what I did — unfortunately. Federal Chancellor Julius Raab, Minister Kamitz and Ernst Kolb, the Education Minister were present. I was asked if I wished to take over as Director of the newly rebuilt Vienna State Opera, upon which I declared: 'Over the last seven years I have been following my plan to build an international career so that I may no longer be solely dependent upon my homeland, either professionally or for my existence. Under no circumstances would I tear up these international connections. That is to say, I must be given three free months in each year. In the course of the ten-month season in Vienna that would mean

* Opera by Pfitzner, popular in German-speaking countries but rarely performed elsewhere. (Tr)

that I could be available to the Opera House for seven months. During the remaining three months I would keep my foreign concert and opera commitments, but take care to restrict this time within the year. If, gentlemen,' I concluded, 'you are agreeable to this, we may begin discussions.' The proposal was approved, an attendance of seven months would be entirely sufficient for the management of the house, and my suggestion was therefore acceptable.

Out of the detailed negotiations there emerged a five-year contract which I concluded with the Bundestheaterverwaltung in 1954. Now I set about the preparations, for it was my intention to open the house not with one opera, but with a whole opera festival.

This opera festival began on November 5, 1955 with *Fidelio*. The very next day there followed a new *Don Giovanni*, then a *Rosenkavalier* conducted by Knappertsbusch; then a new *Aïda* under the musical supervision of Kubelik; and then a new production of *Wozzeck* conducted by myself; *Die Meistersinger* under Fritz Reiner; and, what is more — 'last but not least' — *Die Frau ohne Schatten*, also in a new production, which, again, I conducted.

On the opening day loudspeakers were set up all round the Opera House so that, as at the time of its destruction, almost the entire population of Vienna could participate. Afterwards there was a Vienna Philharmonic Ball, and I remember it well. As I came out of the stage door, a crowd of people formed a line and when they saw me, most of the men wordlessly raised their hats. This silent display moved me deeply.

It was incredibly difficult to build a repertoire, that is, to get back to everyday operations after that unique festival, because the sets from the Theater an der Wien barely, if at all, fitted into the larger, new house. It was so complicated largely because, in order to make my opera festival as splendid as possible, I had to have practically all of my top singers in Vienna so that I could make an adequate substitution in the event of a singer being unable to appear. Now these singers had commitments elsewhere so that, once the festival was over, singers were a bit thin on the ground.

In January 1956, the bicentenary of Mozart's birth, I conducted a Mozart Festival in Salzburg, the centre-piece of which was a new production of *Idomeneo* which I had to prepare almost entirely in Vienna, since I could only have the orchestra in Salzburg for a few days. This Mozart Festival, during which I spoke a few words on the radio from Mozart's birthplace, went off well and without a hitch.

After this opera festival I flew to Chicago for about four weeks. What was going on in Vienna during my absence I only discovered later.* Anyway, when I got back I was

* The post of Director of the Vienna State Opera has rarely guaranteed secure employment, particularly since the Second World War. Johann Herbeck's brilliant period of tenure from 1870 came to a dismal end following the Vienna stock market crash in 1873, although he survived there until 1875. His successor, Franz Jauner, engaged Verdi to conduct *Aïda*, secured Wagner's *Ring* for Vienna and the services of Hans Richter as conductor; but his fortunes, too, declined, and he was out within five years. After a brilliant (and lengthy) period as Director, (1881–1897) Wilhelm Jahn found himself replaced by an even more brilliant successor, one Gustav Mahler. Mahler's tenure (1897–1907) transformed the Vienna State Opera into the world's finest, but his ruthlessness made enemies; this together with blatant anti-Semitism led him to quit. Weingartner's tenure (1908–1911) seems to have been relatively peaceful, as was that of his successor Hans Gregor (who was not a musician). The co-directorship of Richard Strauss and Franz Schalk (1919–24) was a splendid period, and even after Strauss resigned because of increasing disagreements with his co-director, Schalk continued alone, successfully, until 1929. Clemens Krauss became Director in 1929, but after the accession to power of the Nazis in Germany in 1933, he resigned unexpectedly in 1934 and took all the best singers with him to Berlin! Weingarter returned, but only for a year, and Bruno Walter's position as musical 'advisor' (the Director was a non-musician) was terminated at

besieged at the airport by journalists with catch questions which I — completely exhausted by the long flight — incautiously answered in a manner which enabled them to weave not one but several snares for me.

Then came the performance of *Fidelio*. When I mounted the rostrum to conduct this revived performance of the opera I was met with a chorus of whistling that still rings in my ears — it was the only time in my life such a thing ever happened. Then I made a fatal mistake. Instead of starting the Overture right away, I stupidly delayed the start, simply because I did not want to disgrace Beethoven's music, and sat there, paralysed, until the end of the demonstration.

There were other bitter experiences which, however, I have now overcome, thank God, which is more than I can say about the *Fidelio* scandal. However bombastic this may sound, I shall never forget that experience to the day I die. True, there was enthusiastic applause after the third Leonore Overture before the final scene — the Philharmonic played this piece incomparably — but I did not turn round, neither did I appear in front of the curtain at the end.

The demonstrations at the *Fidelio* performance were planned, of course. I learned later that there had been a

the Anschluss in March 1938. Böhm, of course (Director from 1943), was faced with the enforced closure of theatres throughout the Reich in 1944, and was bombed out in May 1945. Böhm returned in 1955, perhaps against his better judgement, but the prospect of opening the rebuilt Opera House must have been irresistible: at all events, despite, as he explains, having official leave of absence to maintain his international career, he was deemed to be overly-absent and replaced by Karajan after only two years. The resignation of Karajan in 1964 was a splendid Viennese scandal and caused something of a Government crisis. The writer recalls a performance of *Don Giovanni* at the opening of the following season, with Josef Krips mounting the rostrum to cries of 'Hoch Karajan!' from the *Galeriestehplätze*. Lorin Maazel's appointment in 1982 was also short-lived. (Tr) meeting of the regular occupants of the standing places at the back of the stalls and in the gallery at which whistles and money for the necessary tickets were given out. When I think that on my appointment as Opera Director they organized a torchlight procession in my honour as far as the Schwarzenbergplatz — they were the standing place regulars too! And now I had to go through the experience of literally being spat upon at the stage door after this performance of *Fidelio*!

I should like to stress at this point that during my directorship, as well as before, afterwards and to this day, the Vienna Philharmonic has always stood by me — which I cannot say of artistic staff in every case.

I have to recognise that those same singers whom I had always helped, whose careers I had practically built and who had me to thank for wonderful contracts, eagerly stirred up the intrigue. They had even dealt extensively behind my back with my successor. I shall spare the reader all the arguments that were supposed to justify my disqualification as Opera Director — after all, I had been since 1927 at the head of many leading theatres in the role of Opera Director or General Music Director.

Naturally I drew the necessary conclusions after the *Fidelio* demonstration and asked to be released from my contract which I must admit, with the benefit of hindsight, was madness from a purely financial standpoint, since my contract was for five years and I had in no sense broken it, but, on the contrary, had only taken half of the leave that had been due to me. I should therefore have had a justifiable claim to four years in office.

There was a press conference at which the mood of most of the journalists was thoroughly conciliatory and at which regrets about the situation were clearly expressed. One well-meaning representative of the press urged me to reconsider the matter thoroughly and to call for a statement from the head of the Bundestheaterverwaltung. The statement was, however, refused me on the grounds that there was nothing further to discuss. The question of my release was therefore closed, and the question of my successor had already been resolved.

The stress of all this caused my wife to have a heart attack, and anyone who knows with what love I had been attached to the Vienna State Opera and its Orchestra from my earliest youth may imagine what we both went through mentally during this time. My only consolation was that I was able to tell myself that mine is not a unique fate, even Gustav Mahler had to suffer the same thing. I had to pull myself together and attempt to overcome the whole thing through music.

Like a *deus ex machina* there came into this darkness an offer from Rudolf Bing to conduct at the Metropolitan the following year. You can imagine how much that meant to me, not only in respect of my prestige but above all in respect of my damaged artistic self-confidence. I never have, and never shall, forget Rudolf Bing and I have shown him my gratitude in what is now more than ten years of wonderful collaboration at the Metropolitan Opera.

I was invited by the Metropolitan Opera to conduct a new production of my 'destiny opera' in 1970 for the 200th anniversary of Beethoven's birth. Thus *Fidelio* comes full circle for me, the opera with which I had my first breakthrough in 1920 at the celebrations of the 150th anniversary of its composer's birth.

CHAPTER ELEVEN

My 'patron saint', Mozart — The Metropolitan Opera
American tragedies — *Wozzeck* in New York —
The new theatre — A plea for Rudolf Bing —
Praise from Salzburg — *Wozzeck* in Paris —
Numerous honours —
The sunken orchestra pit in Bayreuth —
The Mozart conductor and Wagner

Just as I have spoken of *Fidelio* as my destiny opera, I
should now like to speak of my musical patron saint;
Wolfgang Amadeus Mozart. All the love I have given him
over many, many years has been repaid a thousand-fold.
He has always given me the courage, even in difficult times,
not to doubt my vocation. He is, to an extent, the well-
spring of health from which I can always draw strength for
new deeds.

My first opera at the Metropolitan was a new production
of *Don Giovanni* which had such a reception that it has even
been taken over into the new theatre at the Lincoln Center.
The same year I conducted *Der Rosenkavalier* with no less
success.

When I suggested to Rudolf Bing that he should give
Wozzeck its first stage presentation in the USA — my friend

and colleague, Dimitri Mitropoulos, had already put on a concert performance at the Carnegie Hall — Bing said, 'I don't know if the Americans will go along with that.' So I suggested performing the opera in English, as the more abstract parts of Büchner's libretto are difficult to understand, and so much depends on the text. An English translation did exist, but it was not particularly good, and so the Associate Manager of the house, John Guttman — a highly educated man, who, I believe, speaks seven languages — revised the text. Hermann Uhde, who is of English descent on one side and therefore has perfect command of the language, sang the title role.

This translation was an exception, because basically every opera is sung at the Met in the original language only. *Wozzeck* met with such enthusiasm at its premiere that the next seven performances were completely sold out, and we had to repeat the production the following season.

I had a similar experience only last year with *Die Frau ohne Schatten*, the success of which nobody believed in apart from myself. Everybody thought that this opera, which even in German can be confusing and psychologically difficult, could not expect a good reception from the American public, but the opposite was the case. The applause after the first Act went on practically throughout the interval, and the orchestra played this opera with such transparent joy and achieved such beauty of sound as I have only ever experienced with the Vienna Philharmonic.

I 'had a look round' in America, musically, and experienced the strangest things. For example, I went to a college to listen to various singers and instrumentalists. As I was leaving I heard the sound of the second movement of the G minor Violin Concerto by Max Bruch; the cantilena in particular sounded so marvellous that it could have been Heifetz playing. I asked the Director of the institute, who was showing me round, about it, and he told me it was a ten-year-old girl playing. When I would not believe him, he took me into the hall: there, on the platform, was indeed a ten-year-old girl producing these marvellous — and technically impeccable — sounds. Last year I asked a friend who was working as a teacher at this music academy what had become of this girl; surely she must be a great violinist today. Then he told me this tragic story. The girl's mother was so intent on a brilliant career that she kept on forcing the girl to practise, practise, practise and nothing else. The child who, naturally, would have liked to play with other children, had thrown herself out of the window in despair and died immediately.

I came across one other remarkable example in this school. There was a young man who played the piano and the violin perfectly and who, with his unusual musical memory, could definitely have made a career as a conductor. One day, he came to the head of the institution and said, 'I'm not going to study any more, because I've got a job in the garment industry which earns me far more money.' When the director remonstrated with him, 'for God's sake, you can have a far bigger career,' he replied, 'No I want a sure thing. I'm going.' I could understand it up to a point, but the director added that from that moment on, the young man not only stopped making music, but also stopped going to concerts and the opera. But I think I know the reason for that. Perhaps he wanted to shield himself from music so as not to 'fall into an old error'.

There are some unimaginable talents in America as far as instrumental technique is concerned. Whenever you are looking for orchestral principals, there are countless applicants who constantly astonish me with their amazing technical gifts.

The American public, above all in New York which has greatly profited culturally from the many immigrants, has the distinct capacity of distinguishing between an average and a first-class standard of achievement. For it is not difficult to distinguish between 'good' and 'bad', but the distinction between 'average' and 'first-class' is significantly harder to assess. This power of discrimination is either in-born or it has to be acquired. The more I conduct in America the more I am struck by the astonishing development of musical understanding amongst the American public. That is the only explanation of how a work as difficult to grasp as Bruckner's Eighth in its original version was such a success on my last concert tour.

I should like to devote just a few words to American singers. I have had the best of experiences with them. It is well known that there is scarcely an opera house in Europe that can manage without American singers. Today, if you don't count the Nordic countries, the best vocal material is coming from America. I must add that the American singer is the hardest-working and most willing colleague that one can imagine. He *wants* to learn, and as a result, does so.

I'd like to cite a typical example of this from my time in New York. As an Austrian I rather like to think that I have mastered the Austrian dialect, and when a singer in the part of Sophie in *Der Rosenkavalier* astonished me with such a fantastic Viennese dialect, naturally I spoke to her in German, upon which she declared, 'please speak English to me. You see, I can't speak a word of German.' That represents an amount of talent, hard work and a gift for mimicry, the like of which I have hardly ever encountered in Europe.

Rudolf Bing has been undisputed head of the Metropolitan Opera for, I think, seventeen years. The old Metropolitan, the 'Met' as it is called, was nothing less than the meeting point for the finest leading voices in the world, particularly the Italians — it is superfluous to cite such names as Enrico Caruso, Beniamino Gigli, etc. Before Bing took office, the usual thing was for the singers to meet at most one evening before the performance and briefly discuss where they would enter and exit. Then (and Caruso was an exception to this) they would mostly sing their arias from the footlights and take the applause of their listeners there — especially the Italians, for the Met audience consisted then mostly of Italians. New York is still, as they say, 'the biggest Italian city'.

Bing, who came from a totally different cultural milieu, slowly began to curb this 'star system'. He went so far as to subject the curtain-calls to a strict ceremonial discipline. That was a simple necessity, because curtain-calls were leading to unseemly scenes between prima donnas and non-prima donnas.

Above everything else, Bing is such a pleasure to work with as a Director because when he says yes, he means yes, and when he says no, he means no. There is also such advance planning — not least thanks to his excellent sub-directors, particularly Bob Hermans — that I already have my rehearsal and performance schedules for the season after next. In the last ten years — with one exception which was due to the move from the old into the new house — not one rehearsal has been changed.

The new opera house is superior to the old Met especially in its wonderful acoustics. And since Rudolf Bing rigorously follows his goal of offering the public real ensemble theatre, I have no fears for the destiny of the Met, though I have to add that Bing does not have it easy, in so far as he has to go out and beg for his money, or rather subsidies, since neither the federal government nor the City of New York places fixed funds at the disposal of the Opera.

As summer draws on, my longing for Salzburg grows, and it is always a new experience for me every time to see the outline of the castle and its surrounding garland of mountains. It always strikes me as a miracle that I have the good fortune to be active in the city in which (for me) the greatest genius in the world was born. Thus it was that the first work I conducted at the Salzburg Festival in 1938 was an opera by Mozart, *Don Giovanni*, with the unforgettable and, for me, the best interpreter of the role of Don Giovanni there has ever been; Ezio Pinza.

I can still see before me this great artist as he arrives at the stage door of the Festspielhaus in his flame-red racing car and at the very first rehearsal, without any starry grandeur, sings the entire role with full voice. His partner as Donna Anna was Elisabeth Rethberg, whom I had already come to respect from my time in Dresden, where she sang her first small roles, then her great roles, and who later became the darling of the Metropolitan.

In the same season I also conducted *Der Rosenkavalier* with Fritz Krenn as Ochs and Maria Cebotari as Sophie. For the role of Octavian I brought Martha Rohs with me from Dresden. She later moved to Vienna with me. My first Salzburg concert with the Vienna Philharmonic also took place that summer of 1938.

With the exception of a few years after the war, I have conducted at every season in Salzburg, usually two operas and two Philharmonic concerts. Among the most important occasions which I recall and which were also celebrated in Salzburg as landmarks of the Festival was a new production of *Arabella* in 1947, when I worked for the first time with Günther Rennert, of whom I had heard so many good things and who has since become one of the foremost producers in Germany, indeed, in the whole world. Maria Reining was Arabella, Lisa della Casa was Zdenka and Hans Hotter, Mandryka . . . Then, in 1950, a lovely new production of *Capriccio* with Lisa della Casa as the Countess, and Paul Schöffler as Theatre Director Laroche.

Then, as I have said, in 1951 I presented *Wozzeck* for the first time after the war in Oscar Fritz Schuh's production with Christel Goltz and Josef Herrmann. As the publishers,

Universal Edition, informed me, the result of this was to open the way to international exposure for this work which I love so much.

Wozzeck then came to the Vienna State Opera, and I shall never forget the guest appearance I made with this production at the Théâtre des Champs-Elysées in Paris. The Parisians, who have a pronounced instinct for really great art, fell for the work, I might almost say, from the very first bar. For such a modern work the applause at the end was frenzied.

This reminds me of a remarkable incident in Paris. I was standing, happy and exhausted, backstage in the theatre when an attendant announced a gentleman by the name of Olin Downes. I explained that I had no time and was too tired anyway. Then one of the artists suggested: 'I don't think the man is entirely unimportant, because he is the most famous critic in America, the chief critic of The New York Times'. To this I replied, 'I'm still not interested.' At that moment a small man appeared in front of me and let loose over me a flood of English and French words. From this I could only take it that this elderly man was really excited by the performance. Thereupon, the review in the The New York Times was a hymn to the work and the performance. At the end of this astonishing visit he added: 'I have heard that you can conduct Mozart as well as you do Alban Berg; I can hardly believe that.' To which I replied, 'you can see for yourself. Tomorrow we are going to Brussels where I shall conduct a performance of *Così fan tutte.*' When Downes said in his lighthearted manner, 'I shall be there at that performance,' I took this as a bit of flummery, but, to my astonishment, there he was at the performance of *Così fan tutte*, after which he wrote a review equally as rapturous as that for the Paris *Wozzeck*.

In 1952 I was absent from Salzburg because of my eye operation. In 1953 I conducted my first performance there of *Così fan tutte* which was given in the Carabinieri-saal in bad weather, but thereafter more usually in the Residenzhof, with my splendid Vienna cast of Irmgard Seefried, Dagmar Hermann, Lisa Otto, Erich Kunz, Anton Dermota and Paul Schöffler. And the same year I conducted the first performance of the Opera *Der Prozess* by Gottfried von Einem after Franz Kafka. Max Lorenz sang Josef K, and Lisa della Casa the three female roles.

The following year brought a new production of *Ariadne auf Naxos* with Josef Gielen as the producer. *Idomeneo*, *Entführung*, *Figaro* and *Così fan tutte* were the works for the Mozart Jubilee year of 1956. In 1957 a new *Figaro* in a production by Günther Rennert was brought out and, also under Rennert, a particularly lovely production of *Die schweigsame Frau* with the ideal cast of Hans Hotter, Fritz Wunderlich, who sadly died so young, Hermann Prey and Hilde Güden. I had not conducted the work since its first performance in Dresden and was delighted to encounter it once more.

Rennert is a producer with whom, as with the late Wieland Wagner, I was always happy to work. He works fanatically and has the capacity to make changes without losing his own direction. I can illustrate this with an example from *Figaro*. I have done this opera twice with him in Salzburg. I was particularly happy with the first production in 1957, but in the second one he had, on his own initiative, corrected everything that was capable of improvement without having spoken to me about it. I believe that this second production in 1966 — so far as one can tell within the transience of opera performance, scenically as well as musically — represented an ideal solution on all points.

At the end of the 1959 season I received the Ribbon of Honour of the Province of Salzburg and the Gold Medal of Salzburg, the City of Mozart. And while I am on the subject of honours, I must mention that over the years they have not exactly been bestowed upon me meanly. I became an Honorary Member of the Salzburg Mozarteum, I had already received the Ring of Honour of the Vienna Philharmonic, then honorary membership of its Orchestra, and on the occasion of the Orchestra's Jubilee in 1967 they coined for me specially the title of Honorary Conductor. I became an Honorary Senator of the Karl-Franz University in Graz, which I saw again on this occasion for the first time since receiving my doctorate. And on August 31, 1964 — one of the loveliest of gifts of all — I became a Freeman of the City of Salzburg. In the speech I made on this occasion I said that this Freedom was for me the highest and finest of honours, for it made me a compatriot of Mozart.

They bestowed upon me the Ring of Honour of the City of Vienna, honorary membership of the *Gesellschaft für Musiktheater* and the *Konzerthausgesellschaft* in Vienna. From the Austrian State I received the official title of General Music Director with the provision that nobody else would be allowed to hold this title during my lifetime.

From the Federal Republic of Germany I received the *Bundesverdienstorden* [Federal Order of Merit] and later the *Bundesverdienstkreuz* [Federal Cross of Merit]. Oh yes, then I became an honorary member, not of the Vienna State Opera but of the Deutsche Oper Berlin. At the time of my departure from Hamburg I had received the Silver Brahms Medal and as head of the Orchestra School in Dresden the title of Professor. Not to mention oriental and other honours, especially the *Gran Premio Musica Lirica Universale* from South America.

In addition, I received nine Rings of Honour, among them the one from Bayreuth and from my home city of Graz; the latter was bestowed on the occasion of my seventieth birthday.

In the meantime I had won international awards for my

records. The most important one I received — I was the first European, I believe — was the Grammy Award for my recording of *Wozzeck*, and then I won the award of the largest Japanese music magazine publishers, the Record Academy Prize. I won the Edison Award three times — most recently for Haydn's 'Seasons' and the Prix Jacques Rougé.

After a few recordings, 1961 brought me together again with the Sächsische Staatskapelle. Nathan Milstein was the soloist in the Mozart A major Concerto; after that we played Bruckner's Seventh — it was the very day the Wall went up in Berlin.

But let us return to Salzburg in 1960. I did a new production of *Così fan tutte* with Günther Rennert which was so successful that it had to be repeated four or five times the following year, so that I was able to celebrate the end of 1965 with my fiftieth Salzburg *Così*.

In 1962, together with Rennert, I did a new *Iphigenie in Aulis* in the original version with Ludwig and Berry — a performance which remains a beautiful and lively memory.

To sum up, I can state that, including the 1967 Salzburg season, I have conducted exactly two hundred opera and concert performances there, with *Così* fifty times, thirty-three performances of *Figaro*, followed by nineteen of *Ariadne auf Naxos* and sixteen performances of *Der Rosenkavalier*. Apart from concerts with the Vienna Philharmonic, I also conducted concerts in Salzburg with the Berlin Philharmonic, the Czech Philharmonic and the Sächsische Staatskapelle.

I so much welcome working in Salzburg not only because I feel myself so close to the *genius loci*, but also because the singers and orchestra are there exclusively for the work in hand, and the cast remains the same throughout. Everybody feels obliged to the utmost degree to give of their best there. Thus, within the uncertainties which attend every performance, one has the guarantee, as in Bayreuth, of being able to achieve a success that is both consistent and of the highest possible standard.

However, Salzburg has in recent years become somewhat problematical for the audience owing to the excessive flood of tourists: the beauty of this city attracts a lot of people, many of whom simply 'take in' the Festival, so to speak.

That does not happen in Bayreuth. Whoever goes to Bayreuth knows that the town has little to offer outside the Festival, even if the countryside around it is very beautiful. In Bayreuth, conditions are quite different; and whoever goes there concentrates one hundred per cent on the Festival performances.

Before I conducted there for the first time in 1962, I was warned about the covered orchestra; it was supposed to be difficult to adjust to the acoustics, and it was difficult for the conductor to understand the singers. I overcame these difficulties within the first five minutes of rehearsal, however. The advantage of this covered orchestra is, in fact, that the sound is directed by the covering straight on to the stage where it is mixed with the singers' voices and then reaches the audience as a cohesive sound. It is an ideal solution that Wagner found here, especially for the *Ring*. And then there are the intervals of an hour each between the individual Acts so that the audience as well as the singers and the conductor can recover. At first I was worried about these long intervals because I was afraid they would disrupt the atmosphere; but the very first *Tristan* convinced me of the opposite. This hour in which to recover is an advantage in every respect, since after it, one returns to the podium fully refreshed.

I have never experienced a more disciplined, attentive audience than that at Bayreuth, nor one more generous with its applause. Applause lasting forty minutes at the end

of the *Ring* is not a rarity, despite the fact that this audience
has entered the theatre with particularly high expectations,
having been spoiled and made very critical by earlier great
achievements.

The Orchestra is newly assembled each year from the
leading orchestras in Germany. Sadly the Berlin Philharmonic is no longer there, because it puts on its own concerts
at this time and is otherwise engaged at Salzburg. The
musicians at Bayreuth play there for very little pay, but out
of pure enthusiasm. Indeed, they all give up their holidays.

Particularly in my pre-Bayreuth days people were
always trying to label me as a Mozart and Richard Strauss
conductor. However I do not like being labelled, although
there are naturally works which I particularly love. I
remember from the time of my youth how people tried to
construct antitheses between the still defensive position of
the 'Wagnerians' and the supporters of classical music
which in reality did not exist so extensively: Wagner
himself once admitted that he ultimately owed the origins
of his music dramas to the Commendatore scene in *Don
Giovanni*. And so it is wrong to think that a conductor who
is, as it were, labelled as a Mozart conductor is unable to
have the same inner relationship with Wagner. As my
Bayreuth performances of *Tristan, Die Meistersinger* and not
least the *Ring* are said to have shown, the two styles can not
only be united, but I would also almost go as far as to say
that the many long years during which I have occupied
myself with Mozart had prepared me — partly consciously,
partly unconsciously — for a purification of Wagnerian
style.

CHAPTER TWELVE

The Berlin Philharmonic —
Relations with orchestras —
On conducting opera —
Should one conduct without a score? —
The correct 'A' — Music on television —
On conducting

Through Wilhelm Furtwängler, who was a friend of mine to the day of his death, I formed a relationship with the Berlin Philharmonic which was deepened not only through our numerous concerts but also through our work together for the Deutsche Grammofon record company.

I conducted my first concerts with the Berlin Philharmonic in the old Philharmonie, and the acoustics remain a lasting memory. Later, when this venerable old hall, in which so much beautiful music had sounded, was in ruins, we had to move, first to the Berlin State Opera then, when this was destroyed too, into a cinema.

A word of praise for the Berlin audience which stuck through thick and thin to their artists, who were close to their hearts: a fascinated audience which is appreciative, reacts quickly and — as I have commented elsewhere regarding the American public — really knows how to distinguish between 'average' and 'first class'.

At this point I should like to make some general remarks about my experiences in dealing with orchestras. I have often said that with the Vienna or Berlin Philharmonic I begin where I left off (or have had to leave off), with less good orchestras.

One of the criteria of excellence with every orchestra is the tuning. So much is said and written about this that I should like to add a word from practical experience. You can, of course, electronically set an A at a certain frequency and then dictate that this or that orchestra has to be exactly in tune with this A. If the orchestra is well-disposed, they will do it. But what happens before long? The strings get higher, for the strings have a tendency to tune high anyway; the winds are soon unable to keep in tune with them — and it should be noted that the oboist, who after all gives the A, has first warmed up his instrument, otherwise he will get higher in the course of the first piece. Over the years it is my experience that nobody can truly say that he has the correct A. This tuning to A — or the tuning of an orchestra in general — that is to say being well in tune (in every respect!) can only be established properly on the basis of comradely agreement. I should like to quote an example which remains a most unpleasant memory of a South American orchestra. Their usual orchestra layout, which I was unable to alter because of the hall, was most remarkable; right in front of me there sat the principal oboe and flute, who in the course of their years of service had become deadly enemies. Each of them claimed to have the right A, and you can imagine the agonies a conductor has to suffer when he has to spend an evening listening to two tunings which differ by several degrees of frequency.

There are orchestras of the highest quality, which means primarily the Vienna and Berlin Philharmonic, who firmly believe (especially among the strings) that a higher tuning produces greater brilliance. For this reason they tune so high that many singers, who perhaps have difficulties in the higher register anyway, find this practice causes them trouble with the top notes. You can, of course, take this view — the higher, the more brilliant — *ad absurdum*, and this happened once in Vienna in a new production of *Die Meistersinger*. Richard Strauss, who was there — whose absolute pitch, incidentally, got higher as he got older — came to me after the first Act and said, 'Very nice, Böhm, very nicely conducted, but why do you play the *Meistersinger* Prelude in C sharp major instead of C major?' But, as I have said: a specific tuning cannot be decreed. The only way is by friendly agreement.

Initially in the rehearsals, but above all in performance, the conductor must be able to exercize absolute control over the artistic means under him — orchestra, chorus and singers. He must be a continual presence. Drifting off, sinking, '*ertrinken im All*' ['drowning in the cosmos'] as it goes in *Tristan*, always has disastrous results. I can remember a performance as if it were today; the second *Tristan* that I conducted in Bayreuth in which Nilsson and Windgassen were singing so indescribably beautifully that the flood of sound took hold of both the orchestra and me so strongly that I suddenly had the feeling that if I wasn't careful, I would have been washed away! What might have become of the performance then, out of control, does not bear thinking about.

The conductor should stand both *in* and *above* the work. The moment he is no longer in a position to hear wrong notes and correct things and is unable at any time to modify the dynamic of individual instruments, he has lost the game with the orchestra. At such a moment his authority has gone. I know an example of this. I once attended a rehearsal at which the conductor kept on calling to the horns, 'too loud, gentlemen, do please play *piano*!' As he said it a third time, the principal horn looked at his colleagues and they understood him right away. When the conductor then said, 'Wonderful, that was right!', the principal horn stood up and said, 'we didn't play at all that time!'*

Long before an opera performance gets as far as the stage, it is very important to have detailed discussions with the producer and the designer on the style of the production and where exactly the singers are to be placed. That is the fundamental difference between staging operas and plays. A production of a play must ensure that every word — even a whisper — is understood. With heavily-scored operas, even when the orchestra is kept down as much as it can be, this is absolutely impossible. Of course, clarity of the text should still be the first law of opera, but I should like to meet the listener who can hear and understand the individual words in the love duet or the whole philosophy of the juxtaposition of Night and Day in the second Act of *Tristan*. Wagner himself said that it was not absolutely necessary in such an unequivocal situation as is represented by this love duet, for the verses, although lovely in themselves, to be more than just a means by which this most beautiful of all love scenes may be expressed in music.

For example, if a singer had to sing a phrase while facing upstage during a *fortissimo* orchestral passage because the producer liked it that way for dramatic reasons, it may be well-meant from the theatrical point of view but it is quite impractical, since the strongest voice cannot ride the orchestra at such a point. Often just a slight turn to one side is enough to prevent the voice from coming through the orchestra. That is why I am very much in favour of the conductor having detailed discussions with producers and designers. However, I do find it less than ideal if he does the

---

* *Jetzt haben wir überhaupt net blasen* — the dialect suggests an Austrian orchestra! (Tr)

production himself. In my view it is scarcely possible to check whether the horns are too loud or too soft and to notice at the same time whether the lighting is correctly focused on the singer. Of necessity one of these must suffer, the music or the visuals; unless one places a man who is completely familiar with the production in the auditorium during rehearsals who then controls the entire stage proceedings.

What is very important, but which is nowadays almost entirely out of fashion, is for the conductor to have enough piano rehearsals with the singers. The simple learning of roles is, of course, taken care of by the *répétiteurs*. But once it comes to studying the expressive nature of the part, especially if the role is new to the singer, these early contacts are certainly advantageous. It is, however, the ensemble rehearsals that are the most important thing in ensemble operas, where the singers' dynamics have to be matched to each other. It is an important job for the conductor to make it clear to the singers where the boundaries are drawn. It is interesting to observe how many baritones believe they could be tenors because they can sing a top A or B flat, but it depends primarily on whether the singer in question can sustain the entire upper register. As a criterion for a tenor I always cite '*Mein lieber Schwan!*' from *Lohengrin* or '*Morgendlich leuchtend*' from *Die Meistersinger*. That splendid tenor Franz Völker was never a 'high C tenor' (so far as I know he never sang one), but he was still a real tenor, as the passages I have cited clearly show.

I have often seen a mezzo soprano with a good upper register who believed that she could move into the dramatic soprano repertoire. How many splendid voices — I could name countless examples — are worn out in this way and end up completely ruined!

As regards conducting operas by heart, I take the view that only a conductor who is able to reproduce the score from memory — like Toscanini — is entitled to do that. An orchestral musician told me that he once said to Toscanini: 'Of course you know exactly how it goes on, but you don't know each individual part by heart.' to which Toscanini replied, 'very well, give me a test.' The player: 'Write out for me, with the bar rests, the bassoon part from the fight scene in the second Act of *Die Meistersinger*.' Whereupon Toscanini sat down and did it. A man with such a phenomenal photographic memory is, of course, fully entitled to conduct by heart, all the more since Toscanini, I know, had poor eyesight. In the concert hall, I myself conduct all the classical works by heart, because this enables me to shape the music more freely, but it is true to say that I really have learnt by heart the symphony that I have just played.

I try to explain to every orchestra that everything in music is relative. There is no 'standard' *piano*, and I have to smile whenever a second oboe replies to my objection, 'I played the same *piano* as the clarinet.' Firstly, that doesn't alter the fact that the oboe has the stronger sound and secondly, it has, for example, the middle voice and not the melody, whilst the clarinet has the prominent part to play. These are all things that the composer has not always marked, although, for example, Wagner or Richard Strauss are very precise in their markings. But not everything can be marked, and it would only confuse the musicians anyway.

It is very important for the individual musician to know what his colleague is playing. He has to know that he can only play his entry when his colleague's note on the up-beat is already there. Equally he has to know where his colleague's sound is weak, that is, where he is perhaps too sharp or too flat; the other player then has to make an adjustment and play a particular note either higher or lower so that the intonation becomes clean and the respective chord is clear. In music, listening is more important than looking!

Recently, I have also conducted for television with the Vienna Symphony Orchestra, who did splendidly in an opera production — not the easiest one, either — the first performance of *Lulu* in the Theater an der Wien. Just as in the early days of the gramophone, these television music films are still in their infancy, although there have been noticeable improvements recently.

At first they limited themselves to filming partly the orchestra, partly the conductor in close-up and then, at certain striking points, the horn or the oboe, which eventually become rather boring for the audience. On the other hand to go for the method of illustrating the respective piece of music with pictures, as might be appropriate with the *Alpensymphonie*, for example, I also regard as misguided, since it only diverts the audience from what it should hear and wants to hear. In any case I consider tags in music such as the 'Jupiter Symphony' or 'Fate Symphony' as wrong, because I take the view that in absolute music the listener wants to create his own conception. In my opinion one should give no such indications to either the educated or the naïve listener unless the composer himself, as with Beethoven in the 'Pastoral', has given the listener certain clues for his imagination.

A television music production should not in any case be a conducting lesson for a beginner. I sometimes find it very difficult to remain natural at the playback when they call, 'stand by! Take!' You have just heard the piece acoustically and now the appropriate gestures have to be made for the visual image. Since I believe I am anything but an actor on the podium, I find this conducting to playback (which does not require much rhythmic control!) particularly difficult. It is the same thing as in photography. One is only natural in action, when unconstrained and direct.

Conducting looks rather easy, and once you know how to beat time, there's no art in beating time as such — but giving the relevant tempo is really just a thin framework over which the magic of interpretation must be spread. I have often reflected on the fascination a conductor has for an audience. We musicians are all creatures of mood, just like the audience. One always gives of one's best, or seeks to do so. '*Vom Herzen möge es wieder zu Herzen gehen*' ['From the heart may it go once more to the heart'] as Beethoven wrote at the top of his *Missa Solemnis*: that's why no 'desk music' can ever conquer the hearts of the listeners.

In rehearsal, a conductor has to be as fussy as a schoolmaster in order to be able to follow the composer's every nuance, while in the performance he should no longer be thinking about whether the horn will fluff a difficult passage or not — or else he most certainly will. I have experienced things you would hardly believe. In Dresden the principal cello was a Herr Hesse, a very well-read man, whom I sadly lost track of after the war. Once I conducted a Bruckner symphony by heart and mistakenly, through the length of one bar, *thought*, without looking at the cellos, that they should enter at that point, and Herr Hesse was the only one to come in too early. I gestured to him to stop and asked him afterwards: 'Herr Hesse, you were the only one to make a wrong entry.' 'Herr Professor, I had the feeling that you wanted me to come in!' Would you believe it?

This power of suggestion the conductor has can have a positive as well as a negative effect. A good orchestra can tell by the second or third bar what they can expect of 'him up there', be it in opera or in concert.

I have conducted *Figaro* perhaps two hundred and fifty times. Before every performance I leaf through the score and, time and again, I discover something that grabs me. I cannot understand colleagues who get bored by such works because they have 'churned them out' so often. If I had the feeling that I no longer got pleasure from conducting a work, I wouldn't do it any more, for if something bores me, I should say to myself, 'it's a waste of the money they're paying you — and you're betraying your art.'

When I stand in front of an orchestra I try to familiarize the distinct individual artists in the Vienna, Berlin or New York Philharmonic with my ideal image of the score which I shall never achieve, but which I ceaselessly strive to approach. Little is to be gained by giving orders; the only way to achieve such a musical conception is by way of free will based on the power of artistic conviction. If a conductor continually shows his weak points he has lost the orchestra completely. This has nothing to do with lack of authority. I can well understand that a musician who knows the work in detail and is the master of his instrument might say in certain circumstances, 'I know the tempi better than him standing up there,' and inwardly no longer co-operates. That's where it all starts to fall apart; through lack of interest the players even play wrong notes, and finally the performance is spoiled.

One must have a very specific conception of a work of art and convey it in the finest detail to the players at rehearsal, for in art there is nothing that is not important. At the performance itself improvisation or imagination can play a certain part so that the impression of a degree of spontaneity is created.

If a player made a fluff, I used, as a young conductor, to glare at him, whereupon he was sure to make another fluff in the next passage. Nowadays I don't look at him any more, on the contrary, at the next successful passage I give him a friendly smile. We are all human, anyone can make a mistake, and I am now able to distinguish whether the player has blundered out of carelessness or whether it was simply human error.

Conducting opera is harder than conducting concerts in so far as it demands more experience. If I have three rehearsals with an orchestra for a symphony concert — there is hardly even a change of beat in a classical symphony — what can happen on the night? In opera you have to be on guard at every moment in case a singer goes wrong. There are certain types of voice that are particularly splendid 'extemporizers', and there you have to be on the *qui vive*, and that's where only experience can help. I have seen young colleagues who had never conducted an opera before simply break down at this point. Only experience enables you to distinguish between the podium and the stage and to decide in a second, 'can I hold on to the singer who is running away from me, or must I run after him, otherwise everything will fall apart?' Fortunately I have learned this from starting at the bottom, since I started out with music in the theatre and later conducted numerous operettas thereby gaining an enormous facility for making emergency concessions to operetta singers.

The first commandment for a conductor — including, even above all, in opera — is to keep the orchestra together; a singer will always pick it up at an obviously suitable point. In defence of the artists on stage one should also recognize that they occasionally have a hard time too. They are stuck in a costume which often hampers their movements, they have to sing by heart and act often in difficult positions. One can clearly establish by looking at the choir how often their movements make them lose their rhythm. If they are moving quickly, the tempo gets faster, if they are moving slowly, it usually slows down too.

One other thing I should like to mention: you should rehearse, rehearse a lot, but always leave room for the stimulus of the opera premiere or the concert. Over-rehearsing is as bad as under-rehearsing.

As much as I love my profession, there is one thing I am

convinced of: how much responsibility the conductor bears at the performance, for it is here that all the threads come together. He decides the tempo, the agogics, in fact the whole atmosphere.

These days, however — particularly in opera, in my opinion — the conductor, and even more the producer, are over-valued. Of course the producer has to be generally familiar with and make use of all the most up-to-date means of lighting, set-building and stage technology; but then he also has his duty to direct the audience towards the main action and not, as is often the case, to steer away from it. In itself opera is indeed something unreal — for where in real life is there a situation in which two lovers sing at each other for twenty-five minutes on end? This unreality must then be taken into account in its stage portrayal. It is a matter of getting at the kernel of the action and placing the singers in the most favourable position so that they can see the conductor and, above all, sing out! The public wants first and foremost to *hear* voices, and if that is artificially prevented, it will react sourly, and rightly so. On the other hand, one has to bear in mind that the audiences are more than spoiled by film and television with regard to the appearance and movements of the singers.

Concerning the conductor, it is my opinion — be it in the opera house or concert hall – that he should only make those movements which are necessary to convey to the orchestra his intentions regarding rhythm and expression; more than that is a show which no orchestra in the world will accept from a conductor. The gestures should therefore not be made for their own sake but simply to express the way he experiences the music. In this context I should like to say that it makes me glad that there is one place in the world where one has to judge the conductor by what one *hears* and not by what one *sees* — the Bayreuth Festspielhaus!

For a conductor who is always conducting the same works to decide to bring out certain inner parts more than is their due or to make an *accelerando* out of a *ritardando*, only so that people can say afterwards, 'we've never ever heard that before!' is inimical to art, grounded on personal vanity and simply tasteless.

I find that the conductor, as much as anyone else involved in the artistic success of an evening, has to order events, albeit from the centre of things. In earlier days his name was not even mentioned on the programme. In Munich, as in Bayreuth, that was so even much later. Nevertheless, one spoke with deepest veneration of a Hans Richter or a Hermann Levi. Only as such was it possible that, although one knew that Levi would conduct *Parsifal*, Wagner could say to Levi, 'I'll conduct that Act,' and go down and conduct it.

Nobody's contribution as a participant in an artistic success is lessened in any way by his having fitted in with the overall plan; for the most important thing is the *will of the composer* and the *work* which is being performed.

I am repeatedly asked my opinion on the teaching of conductors. Honestly I do not have a lot to say, all the more since I was never taught conducting in my life. Nevertheless, as my time allowed, I have had a few students, among whom was Omachi, who in my opinion was the most gifted and is working as a first-class conductor in his native Tokyo.

You can only convey to conducting students your own experience in handling the orchestra, some technical details and perhaps a few hints about baton technique. *He* must have the talent, and I stand by what Hans Richter said in reply to my father's question, 'how do you become a conductor?' 'You get up on the podium — and either you can do it, or else you'll never learn!'

Appendix

Richard Strauss to Karl Böhm

Garmisch, 27.IV.45
Dear Friend,
   It was touching of you to think of me immediately after
the fearful catastrophe in Vienna. You can well imagine my
anguish. Thank God that you and your dear wife suffered
no personal injury. I have not answered you until now
because Richard was unable to give me an exact address for
you. However, I shall now try to send copies of this letter to
Kammer and Werfen since, according to the latest news,
rebuilding in Vienna is not without prospect, and I should
like to give you with my most heartfelt wishes a kind of
testament; my artistic legacy in writing at least, since it will
hardly be possible any longer for me to support you *in
persona* in the great cultural work you have before you.
There follows in lapidary style (which would, of course,
really require more extensive oral explanation) a memoran-
dum which I wrote down some time ago on the significance
of opera and the future which I hope it has in Vienna, the
cultural centre of Europe.
   German music was created by Joh. Seb. Bach, the birth of
Mozartian melody is the revelation of the human soul sought
by all philosophers. The orchestra created by Joseph

Haydn, endowed with language perfected by Weber, Berlioz and Rich. Wagner made possible in music drama the highest achievement of the human spirit as the topmost peak and culmination of a 2000-year cultural development.

Despite the monumental building of Bayreuth, the cultivation of 'opera' from Gluck up to my own works does not in general correspond to the lofty significance of this most beautiful of art forms (notwithstanding particular individual achievements under Schuch, Dr Böhm, Clemens Krauss, Rudolf Hartmann, Gielen, Sievert).

Despite good subsidies, its management is still subject to a more or less commercial approach and does not meet the requirements which its cultural importance justifies. My position with regard to the unique phenomenon of the Bayreuth Festspielhaus is well known. Despite certain acoustic deficiencies it is, following the will of its creator, the most worthy space for *Tristan, Nibelungenring, Parsifal*.

The Italian baroque opera house is suitable for all operas with the exception of *Parsifal* which is reserved for Bayreuth. However, the manifold form of the entire operatic literature requires two theatres of different sizes; for so-called light opera and for serious operas with a normal orchestral complement: 10 to 12 first violins, 8 to 10 seconds, 6 to 8 violas, 6 to 8 cellos, 4 to 6 double basses, 2 to 4 horns, 2 trumpets, 3 trombones, a tuba, a harp, double woodwind, an auditorium for 1200 to 1500 persons (an ideal house for this is the Theater an der Wien).

For so-called grand opera, a house which holds from 1800 up to 3000 people at the most, orchestra: 16 first, 16 second violins, 12 violas, 12 cellos, 8 double basses, 4 to 6 harps and the prescribed complement of wind instruments. For my *Elektra*, for example, 30 violins, 18 violas, 12 cellos, 8 basses — so, for the *Ring, Salome, Elektra, Frau ohne Schatten* for 105 to 110 musicians, a somewhat raised orchestra pit as in the Vienna Opera which, however, may be lowered hydraulically when needed, for example, in the *Ring*.

Just as the State has created museums of fine art in which the great works of art of the past are presented *exclusively* for the needs of the art-loving people, and *unmixed* with works of a lower order and lesser quality, so, with regard to the corrupting effect which an operatic season (such as today's programmes generally yield, e.g. *Tannhäuser, Cavalleria, Pagliacci, Zauberflöte, Fledermaus, Siegfried, Land des Lächelns, Parsifal*) at least two opera houses are to be recommended, or demanded, for large cities such as Vienna, Berlin, Hamburg, Munich, Dresden. These would play works of the different categories, with the large house, in fact, reserved to hold a quasi-permanent exhibition of the greatest works of the literature in first-class productions with constant rehearsals to maintain standards, without daily performances, being given, by the best artists and orchestral forces which are not constantly being spoiled by being intermittently burdened with lesser works.

I do not need to go any further into the difference between a picture gallery in which, if well lit, a Titian and a Rembrandt do not need to be renewed daily and a *Tristan* which has to be reborn every time.

The programme of such an 'Opera Museum', to which the educated world has the same access as the Pinakothek or the Prado and the Louvre would be exclusively*:
Gluck: *Orfeo, Alceste, Armida*, the two *Iphigenias* in both new and R. Wagner's arrangements
Mozart: *Idomeneo* (arranged by Wallerstein, R. Strauss), *Figaro, Don Giovanni, Così fan tutte, Zauberflöte*
Beethoven: *Fidelio*

---

* Strauss generally follows the usual practice of giving the titles of non-German operas in the commonly-used German versions: for consistency and clarity they are given here in their original languages. Where he gives abbreviated titles of German operas, these have been retained. (Tr)

Weber: *Freischütz, Euryanthe, Oberon*
Berlioz: *Benvenuto Cellini, Les Troyens*
Bizet: *Carmen*
Verdi: *Aïda, Simone Boccanegra, Falstaff*
R. Strauss: *Salome, Elektra, Rosenkavalier, Frau ohne Schatten, Friedenstag, Daphne, Ägyptische Helena, Liebe der Danae, Josefslegende*
R. Wagner: *Rienzi* (uncut) to *Götterdämmerung*.

In this Opera Museum, for the sake of historical knowledge, there might occasionally be included by way of contrast (*Rienzi-Le Prophète*, see complete writings!) or one or other of the so-called grand operas from the early part of the last century (*Robert le Diable, Les Huguenots, L'Africaine, La Juive*), as in great galleries, special exhibitions take place from time to time.

The second theatre, attached to the large opera, I shall call the light opera for short: *opéra comique* in Vienna, the extraordinarily well-suited, acoustically wonderful Theater an der Wien, the birthplace of *Die Zauberflöte**, which only requires minor repairs and bringing up to date technically, is able to put together a programme with the following selection suited to the requirements of education as well as for improved entertainment:

Adam: *Le Postillon de Longjumeau*
d'Albert: *Tiefland, Die Abreise*
Auber: *La muette de Portici, Fra Diavolo, Le Domino noir, Le Maçon, La part du diable*
Bellini: *Norma, La sonnambula*
Berlioz: *Béatrice et Bénédict*
Leo Blech: *'Das war ich', Versiegelt*
Boïeldieu: *La dame blanche, Jean de Paris*
Bizet: *Djamileh, Les pêcheurs de perles*

---

* Here Strauss is mistaken: *Die Zauberflöte* had its first performance in the Freihaustheater auf der Wieden about ten years before the opening of the Theater an der Wien. — *Author's footnote*

Cornelius: *Barbier von Bagdad, Der Cid*
Charpentier: *Louise*
Cherubini: *Le porteur d'eau*
Chabrier: *Gwendoline, Le roi malgré lui*
Cimarosa: *Il matrimonio segreto*
Dittersdorf: *Doktor und Apotheker*
Donizetti: *La fille du régiment, Don Pasquale, L'elisir d'amore, Lucia di Lammermoor*
Dvořák: *Jakobin*
Flotow: *Martha, Alessandro Stradella*
Goldmark: *Die Königin von Saba*
Gounod: *Le médecin malgré lui*
Humperdinck: *Hänsel und Gretel, Königskinder, Heirat wider Willen*
Kienzl: *Evangelimann*
Kreutzer: *Nachtlager von Granada*
Korngold: *Der Ring des Polykrates*
Lortzing: *Die beiden Schützen, Waffenschmied, Wildschütz, Zar und Zimmermann*
Leoncavallo: *I Pagliacci*
Marschner: *Hans Heiling, Der Holzdieb*
Méhul: *Joseph*
Mascagni: *Cavalleria rusticana*
Nicolai: *Die lustigen Weiber*
Offenbach: *La belle Hélène, Orphée aux enfers*
Pergolesi: *La serva padrona*
Pfitzner: *Palestrina*
Alexander Ritter: *Der faule Hans, Wem die Krone*
Joh. Strauss: *Fledermaus* (in the original!), *Zigeunerbaron*
Smetana: *Prodana nevesta [The Bartered Bride]*
Max Schillings: *Ingwelde, Pfeifertag*
Hans Sommer: *Loreley, Rübezahl*
Schubert: *Der häusliche Krieg [Die Verschworenen]*
Tchaikovsky: *Pique Dame, Eugene Onegin*
Mussorgsky: *Boris Godounov*

R. Strauss: *Guntram, Feuersnot, Ariadne, Intermezzo, Arabella, Die schweigsame Frau, Capriccio*
Verdi: *Il Trovatore, La Traviata, Rigoletto, Un Ballo in Maschera*

— further (a fresh thought!), since in many earlier operas which are unbearable for us today such as *Macbeth, Luisa Miler, Vespri Siciliani*, there are parts of genius, I recommend a kind of pot-pourri of single scenes, for example Lady Macbeth's mad scene, the ballet presented in costume and presented on stage as a historical Verdi evening.

I condemn *Otello* entirely, as I do all libretti from classical dramas distorted into opera libretti like, for example, Gounod's *Faust*, Rossini's *Tell*, Verdi's *Don Carlo*! They do not belong on the German stage.

The present Theater der Stadt Wien should be a third stage, and '*Volksoper*' with cheap prices in which all the works except those which are too demanding from the technical and personnel point of view (especially as regards orchestra and chorus, e.g. *Tannhäuser, Lohengrin, Tristan, Meistersinger, Nibelungenring*) could be played and carefully prepared just as in the more stately 'Light Opera' — and not just things 'put on the agenda' for the sake of novelty which unnecessarily burden the staff and which, only in rare cases also please the public, except for lengthy reviews.

Agreement between the 'Light Opera' and the '*Volksoper*' in setting out the year's programme is also to be recommended here, so that the same works are not played in the two institutions in the same year and a greater variety is achieved in the programme for the city's opera-loving public. More room can be made in this plan of mine for important ballet as well as for beautiful dramatic works of *significance* such as *Egmont, A Midsummer Night's Dream, Manfred*.

Dear Friend! In broad outline this would be the artistic testament which I should like to leave you as your prede-

cessor at the so cruelly destroyed, magnificent Vienna
Opera. Let us hope that we may one day be able to talk
about it together before my end. You know that you are
heartily welcome here any time; warmest greetings from the
whole family to you and your dear wife.

from your always truly and sincerely devoted

Dr Richard Strauss

INDEX